RANDI SMITH
on
COACHING ADAPTIVE ARCHERY

Just so you wouldn't think Adaptive Archery is something new, here is a newspaper photo, from 1947. The original caption was "Chicago: Shooting from their wheel-chairs, David Curtis (left) of Dayton, Ohio, and Raymond Hunt of Ravenna, Ohio, will represent Vaughn General Hospital in an exhibit of archery skills to be held here at Lane High School's stadium."

It is entirely likely that adaptive archery instruction began right after the invention of the bow and arrow as fathers sought to give the skill to their children. So adaptive archery is as old as archery.

RANDI SMITH on COACHING ADAPTIVE ARCHERY

Publication Data

Randi Smith on Coaching Adaptive Archery / Randi Smith.
p. cm (softcover)
1. Archery. 2. Coaching. I Randi Smith, 1952-

ISBN: 979-8-218-25776-7

The web addresses cited in this text were current as of Spring 2023, unless otherwise noted.

Writer: Randi Smith; **Editor**; Steve Ruis; **Copy Editor**: Steve Ruis; **Book Designer**: Steve Ruis; **Cover Designer**: Steve Ruis; **Photographers**: Randi Smith and others as noted

Created in the United States of America 10 9 8 7 6 5 4 3 2 1

Watching Arrows Fly
www.watchingarrowsfly.com

Dedication

I read books like this and when I get to the dedication, I enjoy reading most of them, but I skip over when they are too long, so I'll keep this short.

This is dedicated to Larry, my husband and best friend, who passed away on April 25, 2021. He got me interested in adaptive archery and encouraged me to go as far as I wanted. He put up with my travel, my schedules, and he did lots of reading for me. He opened up Salt Lake Archery to all of the para athletes and supported them in every way he could, which indirectly supported me as well.

John Nyland – John was the athletic trainer on my first trip with the Para-archery Team and has remained a great friend ever since. When he had issues with the para classification process, he stood up and explained what the issues were, and then was strong enough to say he could not, in good conscience continue. I've admired his strength and commitment in all he does. He's the one who has kept me going on this project, including reviewing and helping to edit much of it.

Para Athletes and Coaches – All of the archers and coaches I've worked with have contributed to this book even if they are not aware they were. I've met some of the strongest, most determined people in the world while doing this, people who really are everyday heroes! They've accepted people where they were and helped them to become even better.

Steve and Claudia – For convincing me to do this and helping me along the way.

Preface

by John Nyland

I had the pleasure of working with Coach Smith while serving as the USA Para Archery Team Athletic Trainer at the 2008 Paralympics in Beijing, China and later as an International Para Archery Classifier. Randi is hands down the best coach I have ever worked with. She seamlessly blends knowledge of technical archery with a solid understanding of and appreciation for adapted physical education and disability counseling. The interest that she takes in each athlete as an individual, a teammate, and a competitor is second to none. She is a beacon of optimism who is quick to laugh and slow to chastise. I highly recommend this book for anyone with an interest in archery as a therapeutic, recreational, or competitive form for people with disabilities.

Sincerely,

John Nyland, DPT, SCS, EdD, ATC, CSCS, FACSM
President, Journal of Orthopaedic and Sports Physical Therapy Board of Directors
Athletic Training Program Director and Professor, Spalding University, Louisville, KY, USA

Contents

My Vision

My vision for the U.S. Para Team was to produce a team that was invincible, ready to dominate, and absolutely awesome.

Ready to dominate means the team is totally ready to compete. They are prepared for the competition; they have planned ahead for known distractions; and they have backup plans for unforeseen obstacles.

An invincible team is a team that can handle all situations. This doesn't mean they will always win, but they are prepared and can handle anything that may come up: inclement weather, travel difficulties, less than perfect teammates, unexpected results, etc., with respect for everyone and grace under pressure.

Pure awesomeness is an attitude that comes from the confidence developed by being both invincible and ready to dominate. It is being proud to represent the USA, having the courage to risk, the self-discipline that leads to excellence; the integrity and wisdom that come from being among the very best; and the ability to respect both teammates and competitors.

My Coaching Philosophy

I became involved with the Utah Hot Shots JOAD (Junior Olympic Archery Development) Club during its organization in 1982. At that time I was working at the Utah Easter Seal Society and I wanted to find an appropriate activity for kids who used wheelchairs and wanted to participate in an activity with their able-bodied friends. My goals at that time were for the kids to be safe, have fun, and learn a new skill. I did and still do believe in the principle of athletes first–winning second, and I try hard to practice it while coaching. I also want each athlete to do their best and to have fun while participating.

Since that time, I've had a lot of interesting and varied experiences. I've taken a lot of coaching courses and I've taught a lot of coaching courses. I've coached at local events and international events. I've coached kids and adults who wanted to shoot for fun and I've coached kids and adults who wanted to be (and have been) very competitive. I've worked with Wounded Warriors, kids with disabilities, and people of all ages who wanted to learn archery.

Over that time and with those experiences my goals have become more defined and now include:

- To provide a positive learning experience for the each athlete
- To promote individual achievement and social development of each athlete
- To teach archery and archery safety and tournament skills in order for each athlete to use those skills to reach the recreational or competitive level desired
- To provide the opportunities and resources necessary to increase knowledge of archery and related disciplines
- To give archers the skills and resources so they can be responsible for their own success.

I encourage all coaches to take the time to write down their own coaching philosophy and review it from time to time. This helps to make sure you are sticking to the principles that got you into coaching in the first place.

Etiquette and Language

I've found that when instructors and coaches have not worked with people who have disabilities, they are often not comfortable talking with and working with them. They might be unsure about how to act and what to ask. Here are some guidelines that can be used with all people, including those who have disabilities.

1. *Realize that language is important.* The picture that comes to mind can be very different if we say a blind person or a person who is blind. Try to put the person first. Be aware that people who use wheelchairs are not "wheelchair-bound." For most, the wheelchair provides freedom and independence. Be very careful when using terms such as "special" or "inspirational." Usually your students are ordinary people who are there to learn a new sport, not to inspire others.
2. *There's a difference between a disability and a handicap.* The disability might be paraplegia. The handicap is the flight of stairs. Relating to archery, the disability might be a hand that doesn't work; the handicap is the instructor who says, "I can't help you." Be creative and open to new experiences.
3. *Be aware of how tall you are.* If you're six feet tall and working with a child or adult sitting in a wheelchair, try to get down on the same level. You can kneel, or pull up a chair. This makes it a lot easier to communicate and maybe not quite so intimidating.
4. *Ask questions.* If it looks like someone needs help, you can ask if they want help. Don't assume they need help and don't definitely do not try to help if they say they don't want it. You can also ask about the disability. Most people who have a disability are pretty comfortable talking about it. Most of them would rather answer questions and give out accurate information instead of listening to whispers behind their backs.
5. *Ask more questions!* The person who has the disability knows what they can and can't do better than anyone else. Ask how they've adapted for other activities. Find out what their strengths are and what their interests are. Offer to help, but don't take over, and don't get upset if they turn down your offer.

6. *Listen.* Not only to the words, but to the tone of voice. Is there excitement? Is there fatigue? Watch for frustration in both you and the archer. Help the archer learn to recognize the signs of frustration. If one of you is getting frustrated, it's okay to take a break—get a drink of water, sit and talk for a few minutes—then figure out what the issue was. It might be time to try something else.
7. *Experiment and tinker.* If what you are trying doesn't work, try something else. It's easy to get frustrated, but eventually something will work. Remember, not all archers have the same goals: some will want to shoot and shoot while for others, a couple of arrows may be enough.
8. *Laugh and have fun.* Patience and a sense of humor are both very important. Sometimes it takes a lot of different tries before you get it right.

Chapter 1

Coaching Athletes Who Have Disabilities—The Beginning Stages

It's been said that coaches who start working with disabled athletes may go through a series of stages. I've heard them described as apprehension, curiosity, and advocacy.

Apprehension

A lot of things can contribute to a feeling of apprehension:

- Fear of the unknown
- Fear of doing or saying something you shouldn't (or that might offend someone)
- Fear of not having the skills or abilities
- Fears about safety and liability
- Focusing too much on the disability
- Questioning how much a person with a disability can do
- Concern about how the other athletes will react.

As they get to know the archers, coaches often go through this apprehension stage quickly. Relationships with the athletes are important and it helps to talk fairly frankly with them. Athletes can help coaches learn about their disability and what they have tried and what has worked in the past. By asking questions about what athletes think they can and can't do and what their expectations are, the coach and the athlete can learn a lot about each other. Coaches will usually find that coaching an individual with a disability is not that different from coaching an athlete without one.

Curiosity

Once a coach has figured out that the apprehension can be handled, they often get more interested in and curious about both the athletes and adaptations. Curiosity shows up as:

- Wanting to learn more about the technical aspects of equipment and adaptations
- Learning how to improve the performance of a specific athlete
- Learning different ways to coach what they already know how to coach.

The curiosity stage repeats itself over and over; it never really ends, it changes. As athletes advance things will change (they may get stronger, for example) and the coach will have to adapt to the new attributes of their charges again.

Advocacy

Many coaches find that as they work with athletes who have disabilities there are many obstacles that can get in the way of participation. They become more interested in making sure all athletes are treated fairly and are able to compete at the level they desire. This may happen by:

- Getting involved in the overall organization
- Teaching other coaches and support personnel
- Working to improve inclusion and accessibility.

As with anything else that has stages, these stages most likely won't progress in a linear fashion and coaches may go in and out as they meet new athletes and/or work with different sports. There's also not a definite time line for going through the stages.

For a coach who is new to both archery and to teaching people who have disabilities, they will go through the stages both as related to teaching archery and for working with people who have disabilities. It's okay to feel uncomfortable; hopefully with time it will get easier.

Lia's Story

by Lia Coryell

I got started in archery when I attended an adaptive sports camp put on by Veterans' Affairs in 2014. The objective of the camp was to expose us to many adaptive sports to encourage participation in healthy lifestyle activities post injury/illness. Less than six months earlier, I had been diagnosed with a progressive form of MS. My doctors had informed me that there was no cure and no hope for regaining function from this disease that would eventually rob me of my ability to care for myself. I had been in my wheelchair less than a year. I was a 47-year old obese, depressed and quite honestly, suicidal woman. Given the state of my mind and body . . . I was not adaptive athlete material! I struggled with most of the adaptive sports. But archery . . . I liked the archery session. No one was throwing a ball at my head or trying to knock me out of my chair or drown me in the ocean. My fellow adaptive athletes were not screaming for me to throw them the ball or move faster. I had never shot a bow in my life but the idea of sitting in quiet focus and repeating a sequence of movements was something I could do.

I attended several adaptive archery clinics with Coach Randi Smith and her team in the next few years. Learning to shoot a bow was actually quite fun and I enjoyed spending time with other adaptive archers. They were a fun and hopelessly inappropriate crew. I found my new normal with these athletes and coaches. I felt like I belonged and was accepted just as I was. Coach Randi suggested that I get classified so I could start competing in tournaments. I had no idea what this classification business was all about. Coach Randi said that she thought I would be classified as a W1 so I asked what that meant. My wonderfully blunt and unfiltered friend Mikey announced that W1 meant that I was "the most fucked up." His announcement literally took my breath away. It terrified me that other people would know that I had so many functional impairments, as if they couldn't see my impairments for themselves! Seems silly now but it felt invasive to have a label like that back then. And then I was classified as a W1.

Coach Randi pulled me aside and confirmed that the W1 class was indeed for the most impaired archers but that there would be great opportunities in competing as an American W1 female archer. She told me that there had never been a W1 female archer in the US and that if anybody could make the 2016 Paralympic team, it would be me. Randi explained that I now had a platform to reach hundreds of women and girls with significant challenges. That I would inspire, motivate and lead the way in developing programs for women in para archery in general. Coach Randi believed in me and I didn't want to let her down. I knew then that I had a big job to do and since then I have worked diligently to do as she asked.

Archery has allowed me to take back what MS stole from me. Leadership, honor, courage, and identity as a capable adult and athlete. I am a now a Level 4 archery coach despite the fact that I have never shot a bow standing up. I have no idea what that would feel like. I teach Level 1, 2, and 3 Instructor/Coach training courses to able-bodied coaches. I also coach an able-bodied collegiate team and last year they took a gold medal away from perennial powerhouse Texas A&M at the U.S. Intercollegiate Archery Championships. I have enjoyed teaching them archery from the para side. They only know how to string a recurve bow sitting down!

Since I made the USA Para Archery team I have been on the USAT team for four years . . . the last two as an elite archer. I have competed on three World Championship teams, one Paralympic team and am working toward the 2020 Paralympic team as I write this. I have been the #1 W1 archer in the USA for the past two years, as the only female in the five member class. I have been in the Top Ten W1 female class in the World since 2016. I tell my archery story all over the United States so that my fellow Americans know that anything is possible.

Update from Randi (with Lia's permission)

Lia, as of the beginning of 2023 is currently a two time Paralympian, USA Indoor Champion, USA Outdoor Champion, Pan American Champion, and ranked #1 in the World. She is retiring soon from competitive archery but is still coaching and very active with an All Female Veteran Archery Program in San Antonio!

She's done a lot since 2014!

Chapter 2

Getting A New Archer Started

The first meeting with a prospective archer who has a disability is like meeting with any new student: finding out about the individual (you them and they you) and getting to know each other. You will want to find out things like how long they have been shooting; what kinds of archery experiences they have had; and what their goals and dreams are. After you know all of that, find out about their disability. Discover what the archer's strengths are and what, if any, adaptations they have made for archery, for other sports, or for daily living. If it's someone who has never shot, this is a good time to do some brainstorming and creative thinking. Basically, it comes down to using everything you know and learning to do it differently!

General Safety

There is some basic information you should get from the archer or the archer's parents before beginning any instruction. These are basically safety concerns. Very often you don't need specifics, just some general ideas. Some programs and coaches have registration forms to get all of this information, others wait to get written information after the archer decides they want to pursue archery.

Many individuals with disabilities do not have good sensation in their bodies. Because of this they may not notice if they are injured or sunburned. They can also get pressure sores if they don't change positions regularly (something most of us take for granted). Braces and other prosthetic devices can also cause irritation and pressure sores.

Some individuals have very poor temperature regulation, meaning they can overheat or get cold very easily. Temperature insensitivity, which is an inability to regulate body temperature, and sun sensitivity can cause dangerous situations, so it is important to know if either one is an issue for an archer.

For some, using (or getting to) the bathroom is difficult, so they don't drink enough fluids and they then get dehydrated.

If an individual has shot before, they may be aware of these issues and will bring everything they need: water, ice, towels, umbrellas, rain clothes, etc. However, if this is their first time, it is partially your responsibility to be prepared and to make sure they are aware of the risks (just like you do with any other archer).

When starting to shoot, safety rules are important, but competition rules are not. Don't worry about the type of wheelchair, the amount of strapping, or how long it takes to shoot a shot. It's okay if the instructor or an aide or volunteer helps, whether it's with loading an arrow, holding the bow, or even both. Look for the archer's strengths and be sure to ask them what they think will work. They know their own bodies better than anyone else. Let them lead the process as much as possible.

Balance and Stability

The two issues to consider first are balance and stability. They need to be looked at throughout the whole shot sequence, from getting to the shooting line to the end of the followthrough. Being able to maintain balance and feel secure and stable throughout the shot are very important.

Strapping can be used to help with stability for a person using a chair or a wheelchair. The strap can be around the chest or around the legs; it might need to be both places. For a standing archer, an adaptation might be as simple as a piece of wood under one foot, so the feet are level with each other. If there are any balance issues, it is probably safer to have the archer start shooting from a chair.

Be sure to check what will happen when the archer holds the bow out at the end of their arm, and after the release. Archers should wear an arm guard to start with. Make sure they won't hurt themself or anyone else.

Consistency and Repeatability

Being able to shoot the same shot over and over again is, as we all know, the essence of success in target archery. Sometimes when a person has a disability they can do a shot in a conventional way, but only a couple of times. By changing the way their shot is performed, even though it may not look perfect, it may be easier to repeat, and therefore, the whole shot routine becomes more consistent. Avoiding injury to both the archer and those around the archer will contribute to everyone's safety and being able to be more consistent will contribute to the archer's enjoyment.

Getting The First Shots Off

After you and the archer get to know one another, it's time to try shooting. Be sure to start up close to the target with a bow that is physically light and which has a light pull (low draw weight). Forget about rules (except safety). Use whatever strapping is necessary and anything else you might need to get the archer shooting.

Try to be on the archer's level and make sure the archer is participating in the shot. For an archer with a severe disability, it may be a minor part, such as helping to hold the string or pressing the trigger on the release.

It's a good idea to check eye dominance before you begin. Some coaches believe eye dominance is most important; others believe it is hand dominance. When adapting archery it helps to know both as you begin the adapting process.

Start with figuring out how the archer will be most stable. It could be by sitting on a chair (or staying in a wheelchair) or it might be standing. If using a chair or a wheelchair, try to make sure the archer's feet are on the ground, or on the wheelchair's footrests. Sometimes this isn't possible, but the archer will be a lot more stable if their feet are supported.

Decide which hand will hold the bow. If there is no impairment in the hands or arms, you can use a regular method of shooting. If there is impairment, you can look at which hand is stronger, which one has the best grip, which arm is stronger. It may be necessary to strap the hand into the bow. (In a later chapter, we will cover equipment that can help with this.) Sometimes the dominant eye and the best way to pull don't match up. You can use an eye patch or see if the archer can close the non-aiming eye. (You may start out one way and decide another way might be better. Don't be afraid to try more than one way and then decide what works best.)

This is a good time to figure out if using fingers or a mechanical

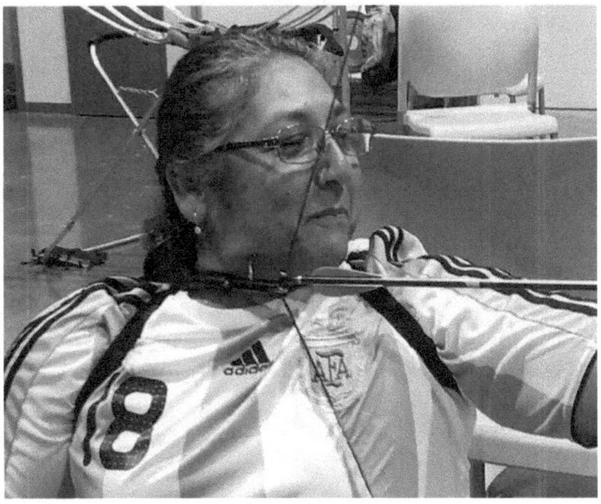

release aid will be easiest. If it's a mechanical release, it may be necessary to figure out a way to hold it in the hand. A trigger release with a wrist strap is often the easiest. Be sure to think about how the release will be hooked to the string and what will happen after the release.

If the release can't be held in the hand, a strap can be put around the shoulders and then under the arm holding the bow and the release attached to the strap on the other side (*see photo*).

If the archer has good back and shoulder strength they can probably pull the bowstring back in the regular way. If not, experiment to see what can be done.

You can position yourself so you can hold the bow up while the archer pulls. (Be sure you are where you will not get hit by the bow, the string, a hand, an elbow, or anything else!)

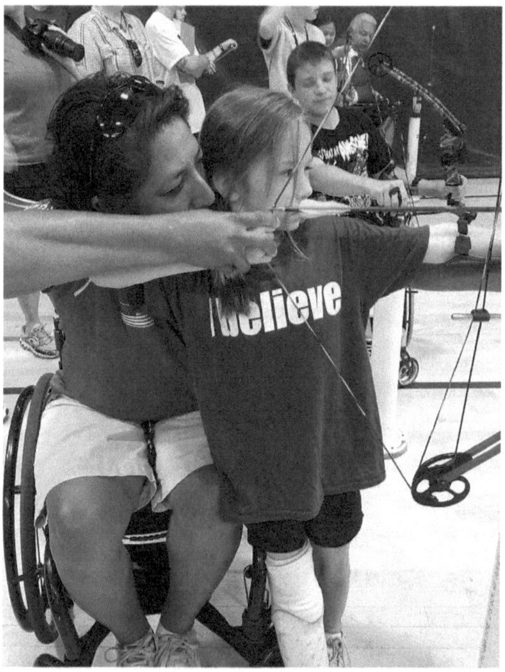

Another option is to position yourself behind the archer (facing the back of the archer). Put your hand over their drawing hand and help them pull. You will probably feel steadier with your other hand on their bow wrist or on the back of their chair. Be careful not to hold too tightly! You can count to three and then both of you can let go of the string at the same time (*see photo*).

Archers in wheelchairs may have to lean to the side (away from the target) in order to balance. They may have to rock in order to get to an anchor. Try to get them as close to straight up and down as possible before they release.

Don't worry about how it looks; just figure out a way the archer can pull. Many individuals with quadriplegia don't have much use of back or chest muscles, so they have to experiment until something works. Some may have to pull back low and then raise their hand to the anchor position.

Check to be sure there are no clearance problems. Check the elbow, the wrist, the shoulders, and the chest; sometimes you may even have to check the archer's legs.

If the archer has only one good hand or arm, there are several ways to adapt (we will go into more detail in a later chapter). A simple mouth tab or a bow stand designed to hold the bow in shooting position may be the easiest way to start. If using a mouth tab, make sure the archer holds the mouth tab with their back teeth. Most archers who use a mouth tab will put the tab on the same side of the mouth as the eye they are using to aim with. Mouth tabs can be made out of nylon strapping or leather. Make sure to check them regularly and be sure to make a new one for each person—no sharing! (See Chapter 8 on instructions for simple mouth tabs.)

If the archer is using a chair or a wheelchair, try different angles (comparable to stances). Some will do better in different positions. Be sure the bow string is not touching the wheel on the wheelchair or the target-side arm rest (most chairs have removable arm rests).

For archers with visual impairments, find a way to help them line up the same every time. It can be as simple as a chair they line up with (make sure it doesn't get moved), or blocks taped on the floor. Make sure someone is spotting for them and making sure they are correctly lined up.

Bow stands can be built for people who have more severe disabilities. They will hold a bow so that all the archer needs to do is pull back the string and let it go. Stands are usually designed and built by the organizations using them. Some are very simple; others allow for a lot of adjustment. Bow stands will be covered in more detail in a later chapter.

Again, at this point, don't worry about proper form or competition rules. Be patient, experiment and see what works. Shoot up close and have fun.

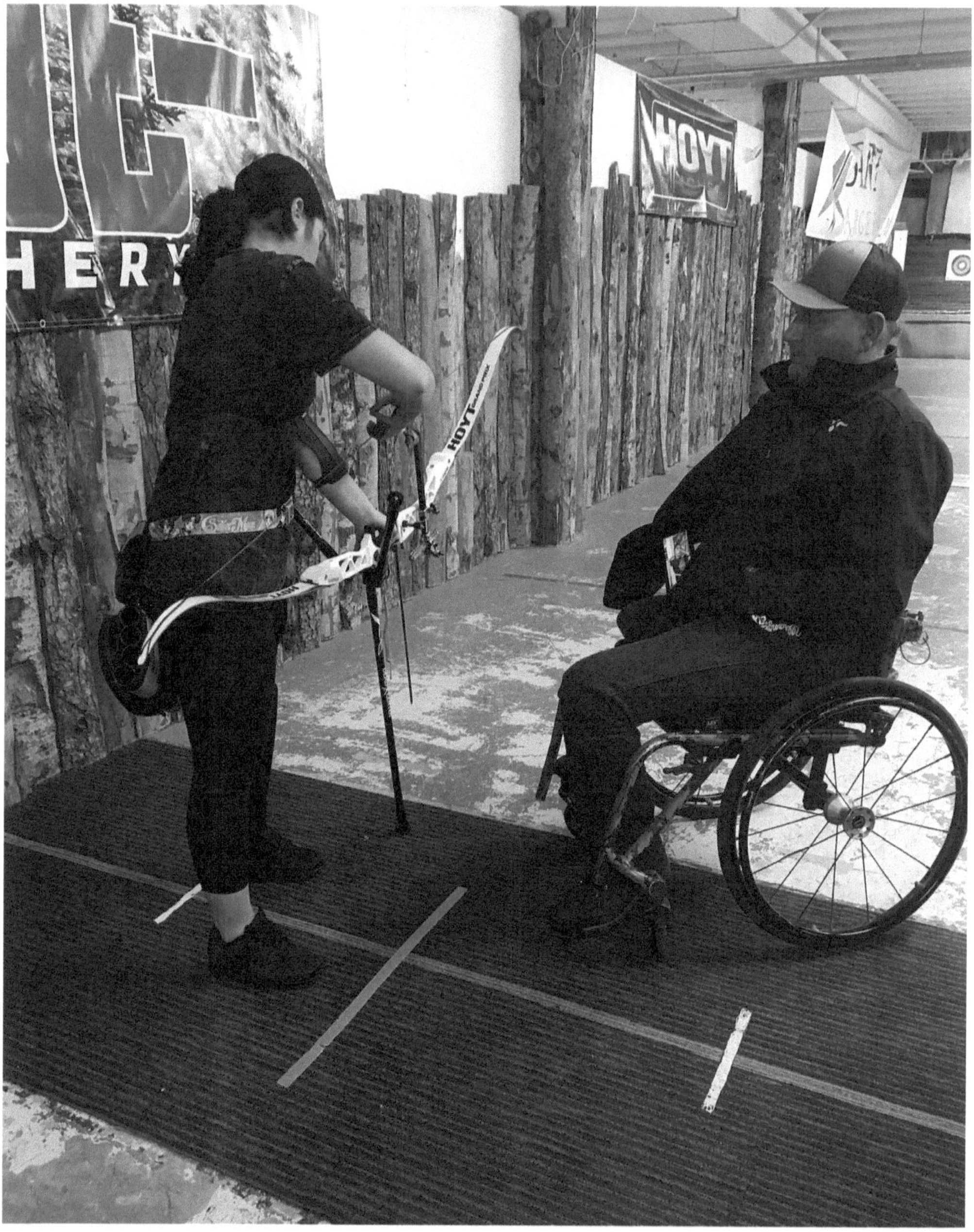
HERY
HOYT
HOYT

Chapter 3
Taking Archery More Seriously

If, after the first meeting, your archer decides they want to keep at it, you and the archer may want to look at more individualized equipment and refine their form. As a general rule, you'll follow the same guidelines for the bow, arrows, and accessories as you would for any archer. Most (but not all) of the adapting has to do with how the archer executes the shot, not with the archery equipment.

Using Assistive Equipment and Refining the Shot

Adapting and refining can be very simple, such as attaching a release aid to the hand differently, or much more difficult and creative, like designing a customized mechanical release aid. The information in this section is for beginning to intermediate archers who are not competing or who is competing in local competitions where rules are a little more flexible. Equipment rules for more advanced competition will be covered in a later section.

This is a good time to start getting a routine (or specific set of steps) together. I try to keep it easy: stance, nock, set up, draw, anchor, aim, release, followthrough. You can use USA Archery's National Training System (NTS) or whatever other system you prefer, but starting a shot routine now will help later on.

Note—Items in italics are the task broken down into parts. Sometimes it is easier to work on a part of a step, rather than the whole thing. For example, when putting the arrow on the string, it might be easier to have the assistant take the arrow out of the quiver and have the archer work only on attaching the arrow to the string. After the archer can attach the arrow, then they can start working on also getting it out of the quiver. This is sometimes called task analysis or "chunking." Each step of shooting has been broken down into parts. These parts are listed at the beginning of each step.

Following are the steps of shooting with ideas for each step. Some of these ideas are for corrections, others are to make the shot easier or to improve accuracy.

Stance and Nocking the Arrow

Archers must be able to stand or sit in the same place in the same position for each shot.

Archers must be able to get an arrow out of the quiver, turn it around, place it on the string and the rest, and keep it on the arrow rest.

- Check to see if stability can be improved. Maybe their stance can be adjusted. Footplates can be adjusted if necessary.
- If the archer is sitting, see if there might be a better type of seat. Make sure the seat fits the archer. There are many types that can used: bar stools, music stools, school chairs, folding chairs, etc. Feet should be on a solid surface and the sitting surface should be fairly firm. Sometimes blocks or something similar will need to be put under the feet. For most people, almost anything is more supportive and stable than having their feet hanging. The angle of the seat can also be adjusted.
- Make sure the stance is the same every time; you might need to make marks on the floor.
- Try different angles (stances), especially with archers who have limited movement. I like to get the alignment from the bow hand to the draw elbow as straight as possible with the draw elbow directly behind the bow hand.
- Archers using wheelchairs will generally have one big wheel and one small wheel on each side of the shooting line, but they may be angled one way or another.
- Stools are usually centered on the shooting line, but they may be angled as well.
- I like to get a good head alignment, but I also want it in a position where it won't move throughout the shot.
- Avoiding head movement is not always possible, especially with mouth tabs and shoulder releases, but they need to be able to get good alignment once they get to anchor.
- Archers who use wheelchairs will usually bring their own. However, there are a couple of things that can be done to make them better for shooting. Start with making sure the brakes are on. If the chair doesn't have brakes, try to find a way to keep the wheelchair from moving (such as blocks under the wheels). If arm-

rests are in the way, they will come off of most wheelchairs. The cushion can be adjusted and you can use pillows or swim noodles to make it more secure.

- In the beginning, if loading an arrow is going to be difficult for the archer, it's easiest for the coach to nock their arrows on the string. As the archer shoots more they may be able to figure out a way to nock it themself. The most common loading adaptation is the placement of the quiver – it might be on the draw side or for a seated archer it might be between the legs. It is easier for some archers to put the bow on their lap in order to load the arrow.
- For archers with an visual impairment, if the quiver or arrow holder is in the same place every time, the archers can usually load their own arrows. It is also important that they have a way to line up the same every time. This could be blocks on the floor or the back of a chair or anything you can think of. It's important that it is secure and doesn't move so the archer can line up the same way each time.

Hook and Grip

Archers must be able to get the bow and drawing hands positioned, get their fingers (or release) on the string, and position their shoulders.

- Find a bow hand position that is comfortable and safe and can be duplicated. You can use plumber's putty or Sugru™ (moldable glue) to build up and shape the grip. Once you have the perfect shape, it is now fairly easy to have the grip scanned and 3-D printed.
- Watch both the bow hand and string hand. There may be better ways to hold the bow or the string. Archers shooting recurve bows will generally use a standard finger tab. As they advance, they may want to try different finger tabs in order to find the perfect one.
- Archers who are using their fingers to hook and draw the string usually don't need any adaptations. It's okay to use fewer than three fingers, or to use different fingers. When starting out, putting three fingers below the arrow can make it easier to draw the string without pulling the arrow off of the rest.
- A mechanical release aid can be used when fingers can't or won't hold and/or release the string. Many commercially available releases can be used. A trigger release that has a wrist strap and rotates and locks onto the string with pressure is the easiest to start with.
- Archers using mechanical releases should try different types. Find

one that fits in the hand and that they are comfortable with. (Be sure to work up close to the target butt when trying new releases!). A string loop attaching a handheld release to the wrist can keep it from falling on the ground where it might be difficult to pick up.

- When using a mouth tab, the arrow is loaded, then the archer bites on the mouth tab and pushes out with the bow arm. Watch the angle of the push so the arrow is not pointing at anyone. Try different mouth tab materials and experiment to find the safest and most efficient way to push out (draw) the bow.

Set Up & Draw

Archers must lift the bow and point it at the target. They must be able to extend their bow arm out and hold it there and pull the string back to their face.

- Watch their shoulders. If your archer can't keep their bow shoulder down, it might mean that the draw weight or the physical weight of the bow is too heavy. (This may not be the case for archers with higher spinal cord injuries. They may need the shoulder up to help their balance.)
- For archers using mouth tabs, be aware that there is a lot of stress on the neck. Be sure to adjust weight slowly. Also make sure they don't have implants or other dental work that may be affected.
- As you work on the draw, you may find that you also need to adjust their anchor (or contact point on the face).
- For an archer with a visual impairment, if their reference points are set up correctly for alignment to the target, they can usually do this on their own.
- Make sure the archer's nose is pointing at the target and their head is in good alignment. For archers with limited head movement, you can try adjusting the stance or the anchor position. This is a good time to double check both hands, the shoulders, and the hips to make sure everything is where it needs to be.
- Work at drawing directly to the anchor, minimizing head movement. Have them start the draw by setting their head and keeping it in the same place throughout the shot. (For some this may not be possible. You may need to work together to find the best alignment, then move the head.)
- Lift both arms together; about shoulder height (nose height) or a little higher. Archers with just one arm will raise the bow to where their release or mouth tab is.

- Some archers may start the draw as they lift the arms, others will lift both arms and then draw. If it's consistent and safe, either way is fine. Sky draws are not safe so make sure the arrow is pointing at the target as they draw back.
- A mouth tab shooter will bite the mouth tab and push their bow arm out. Be sure to watch the direction they push.
- Archers who use their jaw to set off the release will need to find a place on their face that they can touch the same every time, but it also needs to be where jaw movement can set off the release.
- Archers will be stronger if they use their back to help draw the bow.

Anchor-Aim-Release-Followthrough

Archers must be able to pull the string back to a consistent place on their face.

Archers must be able to point the arrow at the target.

Archers must be able to release the string (the method of release will depend on the type of release: fingers, mechanical release aid, or mouth tab)

Archers must be able to continue to hold the bow pointing at the target and maintain the proper position after the release of the string.

- Pulling back to anchor (where the hand touches the face) will depend on whether they are using fingers or a release aid and the type of release aid. Starting out, have them pull back to alignment, then see if you can find an anchor that keeps them aligned. Have them imagine the draw elbow being right behind the bow hand.
- With compound archers try to have their hand making solid contact with their face and the bowstring touching the middle of their nose. When using a release with a wrist strap, placing the thumb under the jawbone gives good contact. The peep sight needs to fit the anchor, not the anchor fitting the peep sight. (They should not have to adjust their head position to see through their peep sight.)
- For recurve archers, where their string hand lands on their face can depend on whether or not they want to use a sight or shoot without one. If shooting Barebow (without a sight), the hand will usually be higher up on the face, but it's still important to have good contact. Using the index finger in the corner of the mouth is fairly common, but the cheekbone and the jawbone also contain good

contact points.

- For recurve archers using sights, their index finger is generally under the jaw, with the string touching their nose. (For recurve archers, especially if they have learned to shoot with a higher anchor, I'll have the athlete draw back to a couple of inches under their chin, then raise their hand to the jaw.) Some archers will prefer a different anchor or the anchor may be different because of the shape of their face. The important part is that it is consistent and the archer can see the sight pin or other aperture.
- When using fingers on the bowstring, the release is done by letting the string slide off the fingers (for beginners, this is usually the easiest way to explain it). The hardest part of the finger release is learning to do it smoothly and consistently (just as it is with other archers). The release hand should come straight back, and elbow joint should stay folded. If they consider "from the draw scapula to the release hand" as one unit, they should maintain that unit from the anchor to the followthrough.
- The release is one of the hardest parts of the process to teach and then to make consistent. You can use videos of correct releases to show the athlete so they know what it is you are after. For archers using index trigger releases have them put the middle part of their finger on the trigger rather than the tip; this will give them more control.
- Once at anchor, a mechanical release can be activated by a finger, by touching a part of the face, or to begin with, even by someone else. Be aware of what the followthrough will be after the string is released. Try different releases and see if one will work better than others. If the release is being set off by touching the jaw, make sure it touches up against a bone; it's easier to get the release to the same place each time.
- Most archers can use a standard "off the shelf" release aid with no modifications, but mechanical releases are also used in some of the most individualized adaptations. There are no guidelines, just trial and error. When adapting it's important to come up with something that maintains good alignment, that can be easily repeated, and that works in all types of weather. It's best to keep it as simple as possible so that it can be easily replaced if necessary. Archers who have found something that works are usually very willing to share their designs and help other archers. There are more ideas in a later chapter.
- If your archer is using a mouth tab, try different materials and different lengths. It's important that the archer bites the mouth tab

the same every time (using the back teeth) and most archers will find a material and length that works best for them. Some archers prefer their mouth tab to be attached directly to the string; others prefer it on a D-loop.

- Adapting for archers with visual impairments is not difficult, but the equipment is very important to their success. A beginning archer will often have someone stand behind them to guide the aiming. If they decide to be more competitive, or even just more accurate, it will be more important that their feet are in the same spot and that they are lined up the same each time. You can use chairs or blocks on the ground to help line up the feet. Be creative! Tactile sights can be put on tripods. In a later chapter, there are pictures of VI (Visual Impairment) stands that help line up the feet and provide a sight that they feel rather than see.
- Compound archers should look through their peep and their sight apeture, lining them up on the target. Make sure the sight's bubble level is level (if they have one). The aiming spot doesn't always need to be on the "X"; they can find a spot on the target and aim there and adjust the sight so the arrow hits the "X".
- Make sure to explain string alignment to recurve shooters.
- The draw arm and bow arm should both stay strong, with equal force on each side. Shoulders should stay down and the body should stay straight up and down (as much as possible).
- After the release, the bow hand should continue to point at the target (or move slightly to the left for a right handed shooter) and the release/draw hand should continue back along the jaw, ending up at about the ear.
- Athletes with poor balance may have imperfect followthroughs; they will need to work on consistency.

Other Things to Pay Attention To

- Some recurve archers who use a mouth tab will use a recurve rest; others get better arrow flight from a compound rest. If one isn't working well, try the other one. For long distances, their sight may need to be turned around backwards (inside of the riser), or the aperture may be below the arrow.
- A mouth tab may shoot differently at the beginning of a session when it is dry. Do tuning after it's been shot for a while.
- Make sure the limbs of a recurve bow are not touching the wheels of the wheelchair before and at release. It tends to make the arrows go very high. It's not an issue after the release. It's generally not an issue at all with a compound bow. There are covers avail-

able for the wheels that can keep the bow from being damaged if it hits the wheel after release.

- Grouping at the distance being shot at is more important than perfect bullet holes when paper testing or perfect bare shaft tests. However, arrow flight is important, especially outside.
- For archers using a wheelchair, the cushion is important. It needs to stay in one place, and allow the archer to be stable and secure. Some archers have a separate cushion for archery.
- The back of the wheelchair is also important. It needs to be stiff enough to keep the archer sitting upright and it needs to be at a height that doesn't interfere with the shot. Archers may also have chair backs that are used only for archery.

Chapter 4
Problem Solving 101

When archery coaches first start out they often have questions about fixing common issues. Unfortunately, there is not a lot of easily accessible information that a coach can have handy to help fix those issues.

These ideas below are mostly for beginner and intermediate archers. The tips provided can be used for archers using regular equipment or using equipment that has been adapted to meet their needs. I've added some quick tips that can be used at clinics or "try-it" events, but underlying issues need to be fixed for archers shooting more often.

Often reminding the archer what to do is enough. Remember, for most people, the brain can only attend to one or two things at a time. Decide what is most important (safety issues first) and work on that. Sometimes if more than one thing needs to be worked on, but they are in different parts of the shot, they can work on more than one – for example, stance and grip or stance and followthrough.

For all of these make sure the archer knows what "correct" or "proper" looks like. You can use video showing what is correct. As a general rule, it's better not to point out other archers in the same group. You could possibly point out (from a distance) an archer doing it correctly.

It is also important to be aware of what the archer's goals are. If an archer is wanting to shoot with friends and have fun, their priorities will be different from those of an archer who wants to attend competitions and actually be competitive.

☙ ❧

Archer forgets about a consistent stance or is putting most of their weight on one foot

- Explain that the stance is the foundation of the shot.
- Put marks on the floor.
- Have them imagine keeping bugs under their feet.
- If an archer is using a stool or a wheelchair, it's important that it be in the same place and at the same angle each time as well.

Archer nocks arrows incorrectly

- The nock of the arrow should be under the top nock locator. (Sometimes there will be two locators on the string.) For an archer using a mechanical release, there may be a D-loop on the string with no other nock locators; in this case the nock goes between the knots of the D-loop.
- If the nock is placed incorrectly on the string, this is a safety issue. Explain that in order for the archer to continue shooting it needs to be placed correctly. If the archer doesn't understand, make sure they have constant supervision.
- If the issue is forgetting to put the index feather/vane in the correct position, it may be something you can remind them about . . . or not worry about it if there are too many other things. It is a lot less critical of an issue if they are using feather fletches rather than plastic vanes.

Problems gripping the bow

- Explain how to put the bow along the lifeline on the palm or on the pad of the thumb.
- Have the archer lightly grip the bow.
- Use a finger sling or wrist sling.
- If the archer needs the bow tied or secured into his hand, make

sure it is secure but not cutting off circulation.
- If the issue is a "death grip" (holding the bow too tightly), have them try lightly touching their index finger and thumb together.

Hooking the string
- For many beginning recurve shooters, the easiest way to start is with three fingers under the arrow. This eliminates squeezing the arrow and pulling it off the rest.
- The bow string should be in the first groove of the fingers, not on the finger tips.
- If the archer is using a release aid and having a hard time hooking it on the string, try using a different release. Some releases will lock on by pushing them against the string.

The archer has a hollow back/is sticking out their butt
- This can often be fixed by pointing it out and reminding the archer to stand like they usually do. I'll sometimes tell them that in archery it is actually okay to slouch. You can also have them stand against a wall or lie on the floor and push their back to the wall or floor to see how it feels. They may notice that if they naturally lie on the floor or stand against the wall, they are in the correct position. You can also have them try to get their hips right below their shoulders.

The archer's arrows keep falling off of the rest
- Make sure the arrows are long enough – a safety issue!
- Make sure they are not pulling too far – a safety issue! If necessary, you can tie a string between the grip and the nocking point. It should be just long enough for the archer to get to their anchor while keeping the bow arm extended.
- Check the rest and make sure it is set up correctly and in the correct position.
- Make sure the archer is not squeezing the arrow between his string fingers.
- Make sure the string is in the first finger groove and not on the finger tips.
- Have the archer grip the bowstring with three fingers under the arrow.
- Make sure their draw elbow is not too high.

The archer is hitting their arm
- Make sure they have an armguard on.

- Check how they are holding the bow (pad of palm should be on the grip so hand is turned).
- Make sure bow shoulder is back and down.
- A quick, easy solution is to have the archer slightly bend the elbow of the arm holding the bow.
- Have the archer put their bow hand on their chest and then rotate it out to the side without changing the position of their elbow. This gets the elbow in the correct position. (You can also have the archer extend their arm and bend at the elbow. If the hand goes to the head, you can then have them extend from the chest and compare the positions.)
- Teach the archer how to turn their elbow. The crease of the elbow should be near vertical.

The archer can't keep their shoulders down

- Use a mirror, have the archer watch themself while they lift their arms without lifting their shoulders (to feel the difference).
- Have them shrug their shoulders (lifting them up) and then bring them down (to feel the difference).
- Try a lighter bow (physically lighter and/or lighter draw).
- Make a strap that the archer can put under their foot and up over their shoulder on the bow side. The strap should be snug but not uncomfortable on the shoulder. As the archer lifts their arm and draws the snugness of the strap should not change (*see next photo*).

The archer is doing body contortions in order to pull the bow string back

- Most likely the draw weight is too heavy and the archer needs a lighter draw weight.
- Explain the safe way to draw back (straight back with the arrow pointed at the target).
- Pulling it straight back also works better when hunting; there isn't as much movement so the hunter may not be as likely to be detected.

The archer isn't anchoring correctly or at all

- Make sure the archer knows what anchoring is (explain that it is where the fingers/hand/release touch the face and that it needs to be the same every time).
- Remember there is more than one way to anchor - but they need to be safe.

- Help them find a consistent anchor:
  Under the chin or
  Index finger in the corner of the mouth, or
  Thumb knuckle on the cheek bone, or
  Up near the eye.
- If the archer is pulling too far, and not understanding, not comply-

ing, or not able to consistently anchor, tie a string between the bowstring and the bow (from the grip to under the arrow). The string should be short enough that the bow string can only be pulled to a safe anchor.

The archer can't aim

- Make sure the archer knows what aiming is.
- The archer may be aiming but trying to adjust after every shot. Get them to aim at the same spot for several ends to see where the arrows go.
- If they are not using a sight and need to aim off-center, put up a sticker on the target to help them aim.

The archer can't release correctly

- First - decide what "correctly" is for the student's level and interest. Perfection is not always necessary or desirable. If what they are doing is consistent and safe and the archer is happy with their shooting, maybe it doesn't need to be fixed.
- Have them get their draw elbow directly behind the bow hand (they can often feel where they are if you point it out) and then make sure the draw elbow continues to go back upon release (like they are hitting the wall behind them)
- Explain that everything from their release hand back to their scapula is one unit and should stay together from anchor to follow-through. In order for it to stay as a unit, the scapula muscles do the work, the elbow joint must stay together, the release hand must come straight back, and the release hand does not go past the ear.
- For finger shooters
  Make sure the string is in the first groove, not on the fingertips.
  Have them imagine painting their face with their fingers as the string slides out of the fingers.
- For trigger release shooters
  Make sure the finger is behind the trigger while drawing back. Then place the middle joint of the index finger lightly on the trigger, and continue to pull and/or gently squeeze. (The tip of the index finger is very sensitive and can reflexively set off the trigger. The middle joint gives more control.)

The archer doesn't follow through (drops the bow arm, lets the release hand creep forward, neglects to keep their eyes on the target)

- A good followthrough actually comes from doing everything else correctly. The string should slide out of the fingers, the string hand will naturally move backwards against the face, and the bow hand will either continue to point at the target or move slightly to the left and down (for a right-handed archer).

- Often awareness is a big issue. After the archer is at full draw, put your arm under the bow arm (where it won't get hit by the string) and tell the archer the goal is for them to keep their arm up so it doesn't touch your hand. I've found this usually works pretty quickly.
- For a quick fix, you can remind them to keep the bow pointed at the target until the arrow gets there.

The archer is too long for the bow

- We've had a couple of exceptionally tall archers recently and our class bows and arrows have not been long enough. We could have used a Genesis bow which limits the draw, but the archer wanted to shoot a recurve bow. Our solution was to get the longest arrows we could that would work with a lighter bow and then we put an overdraw on our longest recurve bow. It's worked well. If the archer chooses to get a new, higher end bow, they should be able to get a bow and arrows that are long enough.

Arrows go right, left, high, low *(These are for right handed archers; up and down will be the same for both right and left handed archers. See illustration below.)*

- left – using off eye to aim with, gripping bow too tightly, pulling the string away from his face (usually due to poor alignment)
- low & left – dropping bow arm, bow is tipped to left, string is hitting his shirt, not drawing far enough
- high – tipping the bow up, overdrawn, raising bow during release, pulling release hand down, pushing the bow with the heel of the hand, tipping the head, too much pressure on the top finger
- right – gripping the bow too tightly, tipping the head, watching the arrow
- low & right – tipping bow to the right, hitting bow arm
- low – nocked above the nock locator, leaning toward the target, anchor not back to face, dropping bow arm, collapsing bow arm, moving face to string, too much pressure on the bottom string grip finger
- scatter patterns – inconsistent or no string alignment, chewing gum, closing the mouth tighter or looser, inconsistent anchor, inconsistent hook or grip, not aiming.

Reading Targets

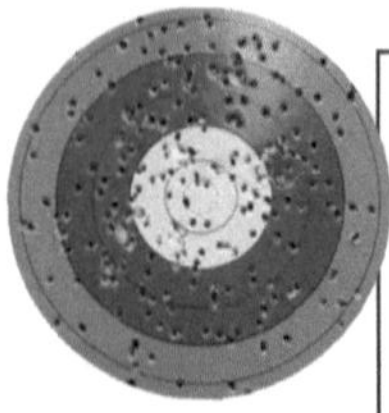

Scatter Patterns
- *inconsistent or no string alignment*
- *chewing gum while shooting*
- *closing mouth tighter and looser*
- *inconsistent anchor position*
- *inconsistent hook or grip*
- *tipping the head*
- *not aiming*

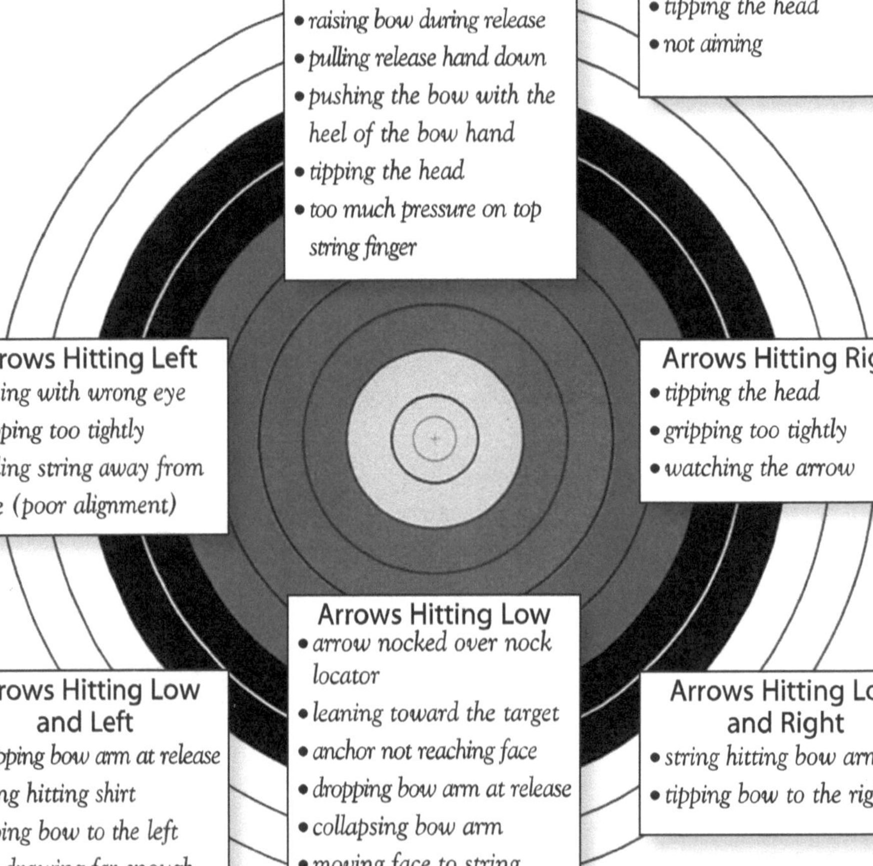

Arrows Hitting High
- *tipping the bow up*
- *overdrawing*
- *raising bow during release*
- *pulling release hand down*
- *pushing the bow with the heel of the bow hand*
- *tipping the head*
- *too much pressure on top string finger*

Arrows Hitting Left
- *aiming with wrong eye*
- *gripping too tightly*
- *pulling string away from face (poor alignment)*

Arrows Hitting Right
- *tipping the head*
- *gripping too tightly*
- *watching the arrow*

Arrows Hitting Low
- *arrow nocked over nock locator*
- *leaning toward the target*
- *anchor not reaching face*
- *dropping bow arm at release*
- *collapsing bow arm*
- *moving face to string*
- *too much pressure on bottom string finger*

Arrows Hitting Low and Left
- *dropping bow arm at release*
- *string hitting shirt*
- *tipping bow to the left*
- *not drawing far enough*

Arrows Hitting Low and Right
- *string hitting bow arm*
- *tipping bow to the right*

Switch the Left and Right reasons for a left-handed archer

Chuck's Story

by Chuck Lear

I got started in archery through just playing around at the National Veteran Wheelchair Games. For a two-year period of time, I would pick a bow up around two weeks before the Wheelchair Games. Then I decided that hey, I like this thing. I went to the local archery shop and we rigged up a bow that I could hold with my prosthetic hook. I only shot indoor tournaments and never considered belonging on a team, especially the U.S. team. In 2001, the NFAA National Indoor Tournament was being held in Kansas City, Missouri. I went to watch and ran into Gene Moe, a member of the U.S. Disabled Archery Team, who suggested I try out for the U.S. team.

In 2002, I shot in the NAA National Outdoor Tournament held in Canton, Michigan. I shot horridly. Glenn Harris, the coach of the U.S. team, tried to help me in my shot process. It didn't go well, but he gave me an invite to try out for the U.S. team. I made the U.S. team in 2003 and remained on the team through 2017. In 2003, I went to my first World Para Archery Tournament. The W-1 team that I was on took the silver medal in the team competition. I made several friends on the archery teams from other nations. I was utterly amazed at the skills and dedication these archers demonstrated. Absolutely no one felt sorry for themselves or tried to make excuses for how they shot. This was the beginning of many life-changing events for me.

In 2004, I made the U.S. Paralympic Archery Team and went to Athens, Greece. It was an awesome experience that will remain with me the rest of my life. Besides being an extremely humbling experience I felt deeply honored to be able to represent the United States of America. I was able to witness firsthand how athletes from Third World countries were able to accomplish such great feats with some very archaic equipment. We as a country, are extremely blessed by what we have and what we have access to. However, we also seem to complain the most.

I have been honored to have participated on World

Championship teams in 2007, 2009, 2011, 2013, 2015, and 2017. I was also a member of the U.S. Paralympic Archery Team for 2008, held in Beijing China. At the World Championships in 2011 held in Torino, Italy my teammates and I won the silver medal in the team round. At the World Championships in 2015, held in Germany we finally broke our hex and won the Gold Medal becoming World Champions. This was one of the greatest moments of my life.

My archery experiences have taken me to Greece, Spain, Germany, England, South Korea, the Czech Republic, Argentina, and China. Archery has allowed me to reach heights that I never thought were possible after losing my left arm and leg in combat. Laying on the battlefield that day I thought life was over. I couldn't fathom how a person could live their life without an arm and a leg. I was so wrong. Establishing friendships with archers from all over the world has given me a tremendous respect and admiration for members of the disabled community for whom the word quit is not part of their vocabulary. I am forever grateful for the opportunities presented to me as a member of the US Para-Archery Team. Words cannot begin to express how I feel.

Chapter 5
Disabilities

This section contains basic descriptions of disabilities and how they might impact archers. There is a lot more information on all of these disabilities on the Internet or in libraries.

Amputations and Missing Limbs

Amputations and missing limbs can be from birth or caused by traumatic injuries or illnesses. Individuals can be missing one or more limbs and they might be missing the whole limb or a partial limb. Some might have prosthetic limbs that they may or may not use while shooting.

Concerns A lack of stability with lower limb amputations can be an issue. The archer with a prosthetic may be fine on solid, dry ground but have trouble on wet or muddy fields. This generally has to do with the lack of feeling and the lack of flexibility in the foot that has the prosthetic. For people with upper limb amputations, one of

the biggest concerns can be determining what is the best way to hold the bow and the release. With all amputations, irritation caused by the prosthetic and phantom pain (pain in the missing limb) can occasionally be issues.

Spinal Cord Injuries

Spinal cord injuries can occur from traumatic injuries and/or they can be congenital (present at birth) such as spina bifida. There is usually a loss of function below the injury level; it can be partial or complete. People who have lower body impairments are usually considered paraplegic; people who have upper and lower body injuries are considered quadriplegic or tetraplegic. People with spinal cord injuries often use assistive devices such as wheelchairs or crutches.

Concerns Bowel and bladder issues, temperature control, and pressure injuries can all be present in varying degrees. Individuals with spinal cord injuries most likely have schedules to take care of bowel and bladder issues, and they need to stick to those schedules. Unfamiliar food, extra stress, and extreme heat can cause accidents and discomfort.

Archers with higher level injuries and some neurological conditions are susceptible to heat and cold issues because their bodies can't regulate body temperature. This can be a major issue in hot, cold, and wet weather. They often don't sweat and can overheat quickly if out in the heat. Umbrellas, ice, and good hydration are important. Cold towels can be applied to the neck and head area; ice can be put in a hat, and the hat put on the head; and there are also misters for spraying cold water.

Cold weather can also be an issue; make sure the archer is well prepared with rain gear and layered clothing.

Due to lack of feeling and lack of movement in some body parts, injuries and pressure sores can be a big issue. A pressure sore can cause major disruptions as the athlete has to stay completely off of it in order for it to heal. It's important that the athletes shift their weight around and move around regularly. Because of the lack of sensation, sunburn needs to be avoided.

As a general rule, athletes should remember to stick to schedules, maintain healthy body temperatures, move around regularly, and stay well hydrated. Cooling vests and hats and scarves are now available, but they can be expensive as well as bulky.

Strokes and Traumatic Brain Injuries (TBIs)

Strokes and traumatic brain injuries can appear to be similar, but they can also be quite different, making each individual's needs unique. Both cause damage to the brain but the location of the injury in the brain causes different types of disabilities. Some individuals lose function on one side of their body, for others it will be more evenly distributed. Some people may have vision or hearing issues; others may have language issues. It's important to not assume that because one of the senses or abilities has been affected, that all of them have. Many people who have had strokes have had their expressive (talking or writing) language affected, but they can still read and understand spoken language.

Many people who have spinal cord or other traumatic injuries also have some degree of brain injury. A person who has had a traumatic brain injury (TBI) may not have any physical disability or it may not be readily evident - but it is still there.

Concerns Individuals may have difficulty with speech and language, which can be frustrating for both the instructor and the student. Occasionally, emotions and emotional stability can be affected, again resulting in frustration and misunderstandings. Coaches should watch for signs of frustration and help the archer learn to recognize them. Coaches can also watch for other signs of emotional distress (anger for example) and try to help archers regain control.

Distractibility, hyper-vigilance, and memory issues are also common. Reading may be difficult. Patience and a sense of humor can both go a long way. Life is a lot easier for both the coach and the archer if instructions are kept fairly simple and repeated.

There may also be a lack of sensation in the affected parts of the body, so watching for injuries, sunburn, and sometimes pressure sores will be important.

Cerebral Palsy

Cerebral palsy refers to several neurological disorders that appear in infancy or early childhood. It is caused by an injury or malformation of the brain while it is developing. Body movement and coordination are permanently affected, but they don't get worse over time. The effects of cerebral palsy are unique to every individual and vary from mild to severe. Muscles may be stiff and spastic; or they may be floppy and weak. Just one limb may be affected; or it may be the whole body. Some people with cerebral palsy also have issues with hearing, seeing, talking, and/or learning.

Concerns Many people who have cerebral palsy don't have major issues that need to be watched for; but with others, you may need to watch out for everything listed above for other disabilities.

Multiple Sclerosis

Multiple sclerosis is an unpredictable, progressive disease of the central nervous system. It disrupts the flow of information within the brain and between the brain and body. Some people have a remitting and relapsing type and others have a progressive form. Both are actually progressive, but the relapsing and remitting form has symptoms that show up and then might disappear, while the progressive type results in worsening of symptoms from the onset.

Concerns Because it is a progressive condition, the body and what it can or can't do is constantly changing, so an adaptation that worked last week may not work this week. Emotional changes (mood swings, uncontrollable laughing or crying), temperature issues, weakness, dizziness, bladder and bowel issues, cognitive (focus, processing, problem solving) issues are things to watch for and be aware of. You may also need to be aware of everything mentioned under spinal cord injuries and traumatic brain injuries.

Vision and Hearing Impairments

Vision and hearing impairments can be present at birth, can be caused by accidents, or can be due to aging. Both can range from mild to severe. Adaptive aids can include glasses and hearing aids.

Concerns The biggest concern with both is communication, starting with finding out how much impairment there is.

Other

The following conditions often occur without concurrent physical disabilities, but some adapting may be necessary. Here are some of the concerns and ideas that might help.

Autism and ADHD Autism and ADHD (or ADD) are two very different conditions, that both occur on a spectrum from mild to severe, and may or may not occur with other disabilities. The adaptations for both are similar. It's usually best to start with individual lessons, so the instructor and student can get to know each other. Using a very definite routine will help a lot. That routine can start as soon as the student comes in the door—putting up their coat, getting safety equipment, finding their bow and arrows. Lines on the floor can help with feet placement. A definite shooting routine, written down, and hung on the wall is also helpful. Very often, once they know the routine and the process, individuals with ADHD or autism can be included in regular classes, where the routine is similar. If something is going to be different or change, be sure to let them know ahead of time.

Post-Traumatic Stress (encountered working with veterans or others who have experienced trauma) Post traumatic stress (PTS) is very common in veterans who have disabilities. It also can be a result of other traumatic events (car accidents, abuse, etc.). The most important things to be aware of are knowing what the triggers are for the individual and how they react to those triggers. A trigger could be a loud noise, which could cause anxiety and fear or it could be something less obvious such as a smell or a voice. Some people with PTS may use archery to get away from people, others may use it as intentional socializing. The best idea is to talk with the individual and have them help you know what to be aware of. Many people with PTS are hyper-vigilant (always on "the lookout"), and they may have trouble with emotional control, and may be easily distracted.

Chapter 6
Adaptations

In the next several chapters we are going to look at more specific disabilities and ways to adapt for them. We'll look at upper body limitations, lower body limitations, and using a mouth tab. Most coaches are looking for specific prescriptions, but instead what is needed is flexibility. An adaptation that works quite well for one archer may not be acceptable to another in the very same situation. There are no hard and fast rules, other than communication is vital. Let your charges know that they do not have to accept any suggestion and that their participation is essential to finding a successful way for them to participate.

Information on how to get started as well as competition rules regarding adaptations are included.

Note—You will find the terms adaption and adaptation to be used interchanagably. Language experts say that adaptation is the far more used term, but you will see both. And adaption/adaptation in this context is "the process of making something suitable for a particular purpose."

Chapter 7
Shooting with a Mouth Tab

Shooting with a mouth tab is an easy way for someone who can only use one arm or hand to try archery. Mouth tabs are inexpensive and quick to put together. I've included two ways to make a mouth tab: a basic, simple "try-me" mouth tab that is easy to put on and take off the bowstring and a mouth tab that is actually attached to the string. (These are not the only ways to make mouth tabs, but they've worked for me.)

The "try-me" mouth tab is easy to make so it can be made in advance and used in clinics and group classes as well as in individual lessons. The archer can keep the mouth tab after the session, maybe as a souvenir or to bring back for the next lesson. (Be sure to use a new mouth tab for each individual!)

As a coach trainer, I urge you try shooting with a mouth tab. When I tried it, I was surprised at how much the neck muscles were used, but I was able to get pretty accurate . . . at 10 meters with a 15 pound bow!

As with any new archer, it's important that you get to know the archer and explain what is going to happen. Make sure the archer has original teeth, not dentures or implants. Shooting with a mouth tab won't hurt original teeth, but might put too much pressure on implants or dentures. For most people, it's actually harder on the neck than on the teeth.

First Time Shooting

These are the steps for helping an archer shoot with a mouth tab for the first time. These steps are for an archer who is shooting a right handed bow, with the bow in the left hand (reverse if necessary). I prefer to start with a blank bale (no target) at no more than 10 yards/meters.

I prefer to start with a light (physical weight) recurve bow while the archer figures out what is going on. For an archer who has enough strength in their bow arm, a *Genesis* compound bow can also work. A *Genesis* bow is also a good second step if the archer can handle the light recurve.

1. Start with the simple mouth tab and a light poundage bow. I suggest no more than 15 pounds of draw. Archers may move up in weight fairly quickly, but it's important to start very light.
2. Line up straddling the shooting line, no more than 10 yards/meters from the target. Use a similar stance to that of an archer without a disability. An archer using a wheelchair or a chair straddles the line with the wheelchair or chair.
3. Have the archer grip the bow with their left hand; the coach can put the arrow on the string and the rest.
4. The archer bites the mouth tab with the molars on the right side of the mouth. Continuing to bite down, the archer pushes the bow out toward the target.
5. After reaching full extension, the archer aims at the center of the target and releases the arrow by opening the bottom jaw. (If the archer does not get to full extension on the first shot, don't be too concerned; the first shot can be scary. Once the archer is familiar with the process, full extension should get easier.)
6. The bow arm continues to point at the target.

After the first few shots and once the archer is comfortable with the routine, go ahead and put up something to aim at. Have the archer aim at the same spot until they are able to get a group. (The group may not be on the aiming spot.). Once there is a group, then the archer can adjust their aiming.

It's also okay to add a sight and/or a stabilizer as soon as the archer is comfortable with using the mouth tab. However, be sure that the physical weight of the bow does not become too much for the archer. You can also increase the distance as the archer becomes more comfortable.

At this point, I also try (with the archer) to figure out how they can load their own arrows. They can set the bow on their lap or rest it on the stabilizer. If the archer has some use of the other arm, it may be able to help stabilize the bow while it is loaded. It may not be fast, but it will enable the archer to shoot on their own. They may still need someone to pull their arrows, but other archers are usually very willing to help out.

For some archers, this will be all the instruction they want or need. If they are going to purchase a bow of their own, they may want to put on a more permanent mouth tab (see instructions in Chapter 9).

For Those Who Want to Be Competitive or Improve Their Skill You Can Do the Following:

1. Help the archer develop a routine. The steps will be similar to those for any archer, but they might be in a different order.
2. It is important that the mouth tab is placed on the same teeth every time and the bite should be the same. Eric Bennett said, "The biggest suggestion I can make is to be extremely consistent in biting the tab. In recent years I have seen some real crazy arrow flight when I don't take the time to get the tab on my teeth the same way every time."
3. A second point of reference will help. If the string angle allows, a nose touch on the string is good.
4. Make sure the bow arm shoulder is down and in proper alignment. The arm should be fully extended, strong, but relaxed.
5. Pay attention to the bow hand. For some archers as they extend the bow arm, the hand will move. It's best if it can stay in one spot through the whole shot, but if not, the archer needs to be sure to check it while at full draw and keep it in the same spot from shot to shot.
6. Make sure the right shoulder (the one not holding the bow) is also set. Back and down is also good for it. Check the final alignment and make sure the shoulders, the head, and the bow are aligned with each other. (*Note* If the archer has no control of this side of the body (perhaps due to a stroke), make sure the non-used arm is stable and out of the way. A strap around the body and the arm or keeping the hand in a pocket are two options.
7. Once the extension of the bow arm begins, the head needs to stay in one spot, or any movement should be minimal.
8. When releasing the string, the head movement should be minimal. Rather than opening the mouth and letting the string "pop" out, it is better to relax the jaw and let the string slide out, or open the bottom jaw keeping the rest of the head stationery. It is important that the method of release is the same every time.
9. Remember to keep the bow arm strong and pointing at the target. The archer should follow the same steps in the same order every time.

Equipment Set Up and Tuning with a Mouth Tab

For indoor shooting, the mouth tab can be either above or below the arrow, whichever will tune and group best. For outdoor shooting, because of the distance, the mouth tab will need to be above the arrow.

Some archers prefer to have the mouth tab directly on the string; others prefer to tie it on to a D-loop. This is a personal preference. Mouth tabs that are placed on a D-loop can be made in advance so they can be easily replaced. Different archers also prefer different materials. Some use nylon pet leash; others may use climbing rope; some use leather. Don't be shy about experimenting to see what works best.

Draw length is critical. It may take some work to get it perfect, but it will be worth it. Jeff Fabry said "Arrows impacting on the target tell me if my draw length is correct. Arrows going left of my group, draw length is too long. Arrows right of my group, draw length too short."

Nock fit on the string is also critical. If the nock is too tight, as the bow is drawn back the arrow will lift off of the rest. Re-serve the string with smaller serving material and eliminate the pinch or find a nock with a larger groove.

Having a mouth tab on the string (no matter which way it is attached) will slow it down - remember grouping is more important than speed! Jeff's comment was "One day I was in the shop and needed to tie on a new tab. After removing the tab I had a friend shoot my bow through the chronograph (using an ordinary finger tab). We were shocked to see an increase in arrow speed of 25 fps."

Depending on the material the mouth tab is made with, it may absorb a lot of saliva and get heavier as the archer shoots. Be sure to do tuning once the tab is fully soaked; as the weight of the tab will affect arrow flight.

Chapter 8
Building a Simple "Try Me" Mouth Tab

This mouth tab is quick and easy to make. If you are doing a clinic, you can make several ahead of time. The athlete can take the mouth tab after they finish, either as a souvenir, or to bring back next time. Be sure to use a new one for each archer (for reasons of hygiene).

Materials

550 Parachute Cord (or something similar)
Ruler
Needle & Thread (heavy duty thread or fishing line)

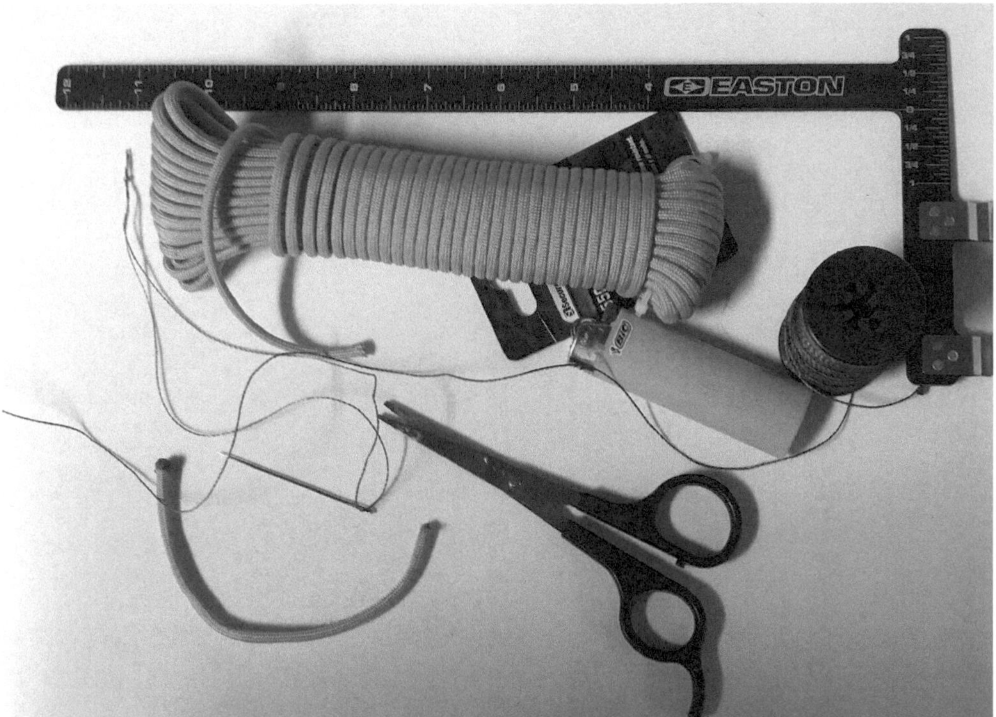

Scissors
Lighter

Instructions

- Cut cord to 5″ and melt the ends with the lighter.

- Fold the cord in half. Match the ends and sew them together up about 1″. Use the lighter to melt the ends together (*see photos*).

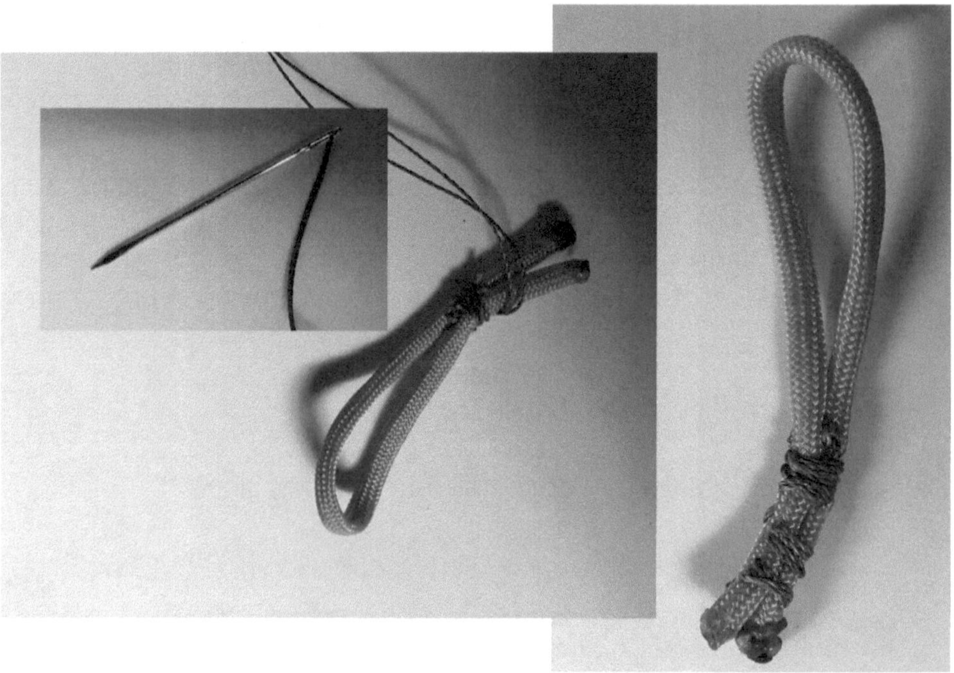

- Loop the ends of the cord around the string and through the loop. The mouth tab will go above the nock locator; the arrow will go below the nock locator (*see photos*).

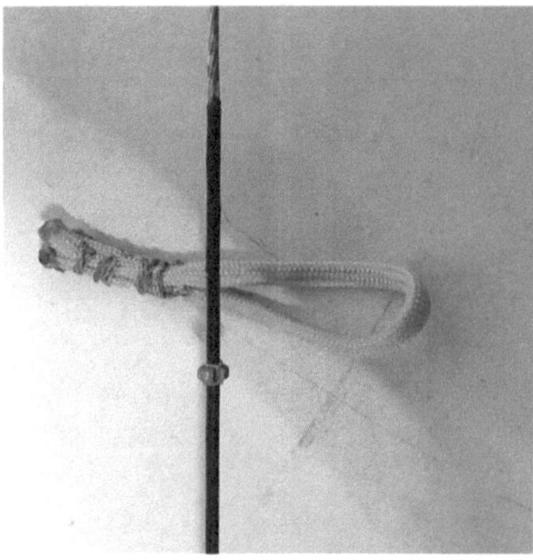

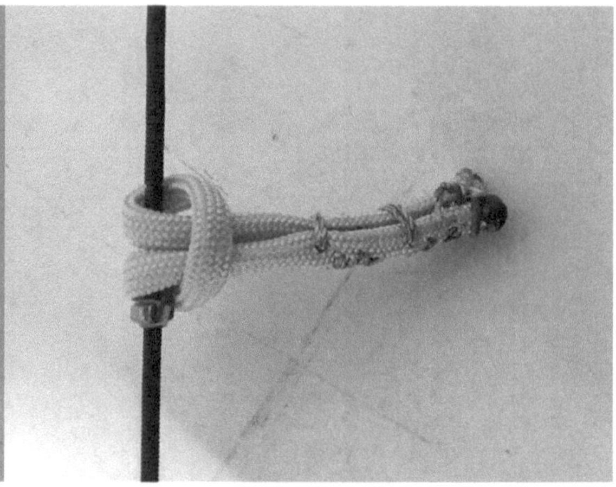

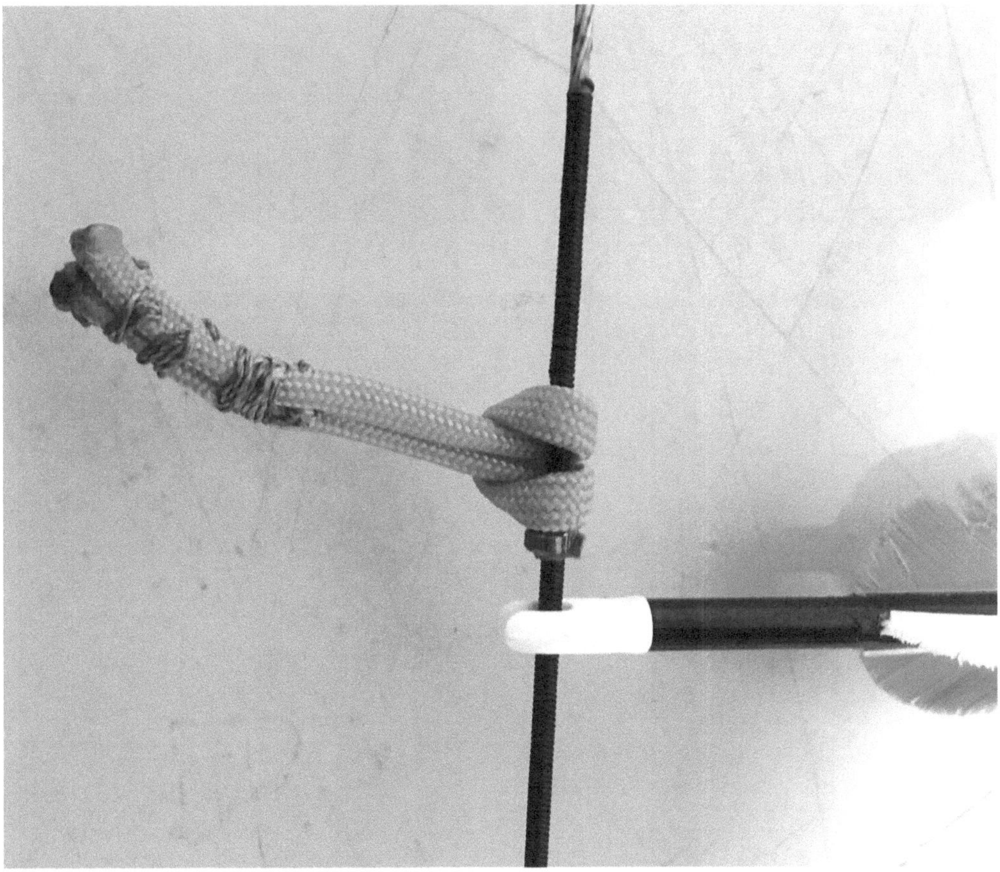

Chapter 9
Building a More Permanent Mouth Tab

This set of instructions for building a more permanent mouth tab; one that is sewn onto the bowstring or a D-loop.

Materials Needed

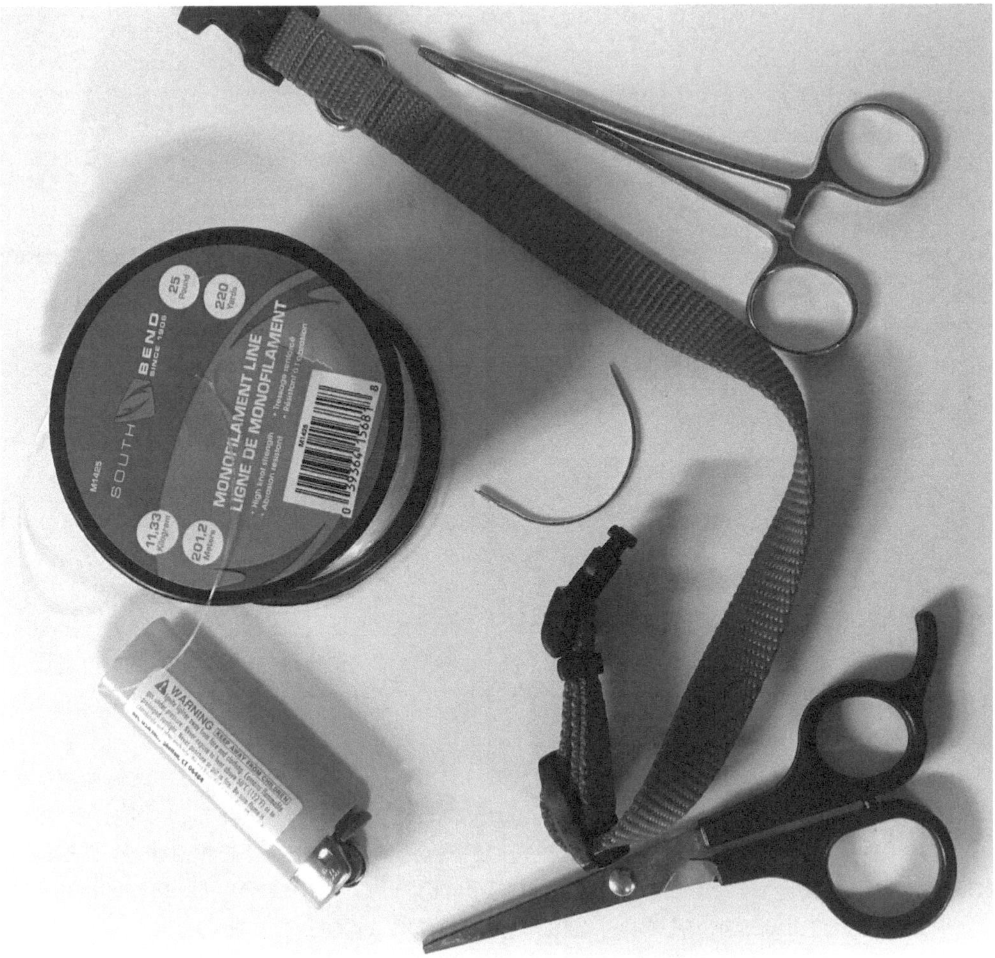

½″ braided dog leash or ¼″ climbing rope
Spyder wire (fishing line) or heavy duty thread
Upholstery needle or other large heavy duty needle
Scissors
Lighter
Small Clamp

Instructions

- Decide where the mouth tab will go by measuring for the nocking point and clamping on a metal nocking point locator. (The nocking point can be tied on if you prefer.) The arrow will go below the nocking point; the mouth tab will go above the nocking point (*see last photo*).
- Fold the material (this is for the dog leash material, see below for "other" materials) over the bowstring and clamp it out about 1.5″ from the bowstring.
- Sew the two layers of the mouth tab together. Begin next to the string at the bottom, go up alongside the string, then around the perimeter. Back at the beginning go up along the string again about halfway and then down the center. Be sure to knot the thread tightly at the beginning and the end (*see next photos*).

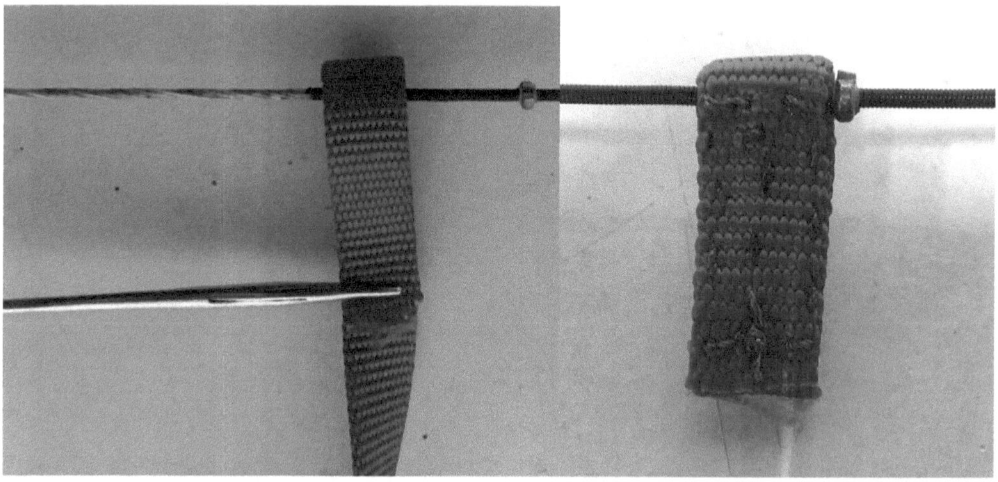

- Cut the dog leash just past the sewing and melt the ends so it won't fray. Be sure to avoid melting or burning your sewing stitches (*see next photo*).
- When using climbing rope or other materials, the process will be similar although sewing the two sides together will be different.

Note 1 The dog leash material is recommended because the dog leash needs to be strong enough to handle a strong dog pulling on them. This makes it strong enough to be used on a bow. Ordinary

braided strapping material that you might find at a fabric store may not be strong enough or abrasion resistant enough. Climbing rope is also strong enough, but make sure it is actual climbing rope.

Note 2 Some people prefer to tie the mouth tab onto their D-loop. That way new mouth tabs can be made ahead of time and quickly replaced if necessary.

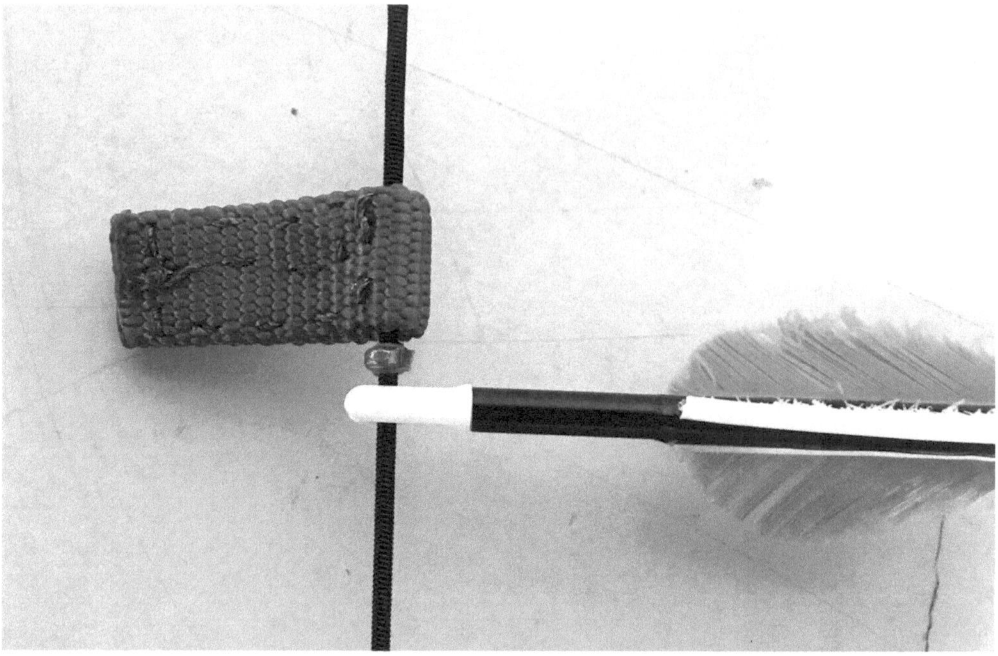

Chapter 10
Upper Body Adaptations

In the previous chapters, I wrote about coaching archers who shoot with mouth tabs. It's an easy, inexpensive way to start an archer who can't shoot with both arms, but some archers would rather use a method that isn't as hard on the neck or teeth. With normal teeth, and no neck injury, shooting with a mouth tab is safe, but with tooth implants, false teeth, or a neck injury, it's not a good choice for the heavier bows and the draw weights needed for competition.

Another easy option is to use a mechanical release aid. For some, a release with a wrist strap is all that is needed. It might be held differently and a method for activating it might take some creativity, but it's often an easy adaptation. There are so many different releases and different styles of releases that it's a good idea to try a few to find what works best.

A strap to hold the release can be made with webbing. The strap can go around the shoulders, the elbow, the chest, or a combination. An easy start up version for a person with partial arms or nubs uses a strap that goes around the shoulders and under one arm and a release with a wrist strap is attached to it. The release is set off by touching it to the jaw (*see photo immediately above*).

Photos are included showing some straps that archers have come up with. Make sure the strap is the right size and is secure and then, if necessary, find a release that can be set off by touching it against the jawbone and moving the jawbone or the tongue.

Lance Thornton uses a release that he attaches to the end of his prosthetic arm (*see photos*). The arm has a plastic guard at the elbow to keep his elbow from sliding. The prosthesis locks onto a sleeve he has over his arm and the release is attached to a connector that locks into a fitting at the end of the prosthesis. (The connector and fitting are readily available.) He has the connector and the fitting marked so he can line them up the same every time. He pulls back and anchors on his face and sets off the release by moving his jawbone. Lance has a video in the Adaptive Sports Series put together by Disabled Sports USA and USA Archery (You can view it here.) (https://www.youtube.com/watch?v=D-c4hTcUcDk&list=PLK7Q-wuzL25xm8yOglKjbFIc2Rt0whPpSw). Still photo (*below*) is from Tri Huynh.

Photo by Tri Huynh

Keith Sekora uses a shoulder release that is attached to a harness he put together with some prosthetic professionals (from Fabtech Systems). Keith uses a bicycle brake cable which is attached to the release. He holds the bow in his right hand and the end of the brake cable in his left hand. (The cable runs up along the side of the shoulder harness.) He draws the bow and anchors and when he's ready, he slowly squeezes on the release lever. Mitchell Miles uses a shoulder release made by the same company, but he releases using a clothes pin in his mouth. There is a video of Keith by Fabtech Systems at (you can view it here https://www.fabtechsystems.com/wordpress/2017/05/chasing-an-olympic-dream-with-the-pde-brace-by-fabtech-systems/ here). Still photo (*below*) is from Tri Huynh.

Other than the harness itself, all the pieces of Keith's release are available over the counter at bike shops, hardware stores, and archery retailers. This is an important consideration; it means that all the parts are easily replaceable if they happen to break.

Harnesses can be made using other materials as well, including heavy fabric and leather. With a shoulder harness, it's important that the harness fits correctly so it doesn't move or wiggle; it also needs to not cause any excess pressure or discomfort. Strapping should hold it securely in place. Most archers will share their designs and will often help build them as well. Occupational therapists and prosthetists can also help build them.

If the release needs to be held in a hand, a glove can be modified to help hold it. Baseball batting gloves work well as do football gloves. They both have straps on the wrist to help hold the gloves tight. Hooks or rivets can be put in the finger of the glove and another hook or button put at the wrist. The release is then put in the hand, and the fingers are pulled up over the release and secured at the wrist (see *photos below*)

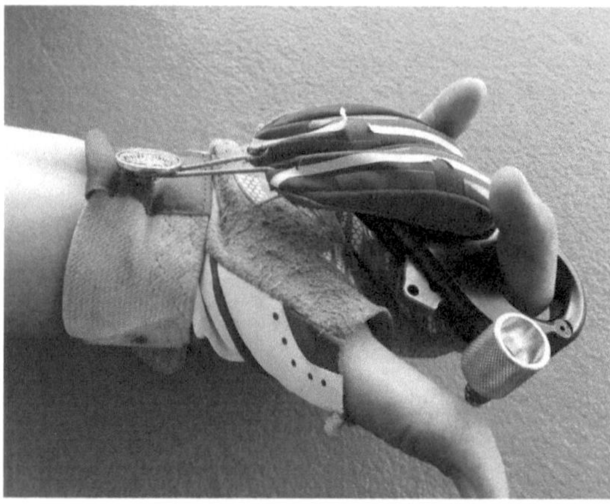
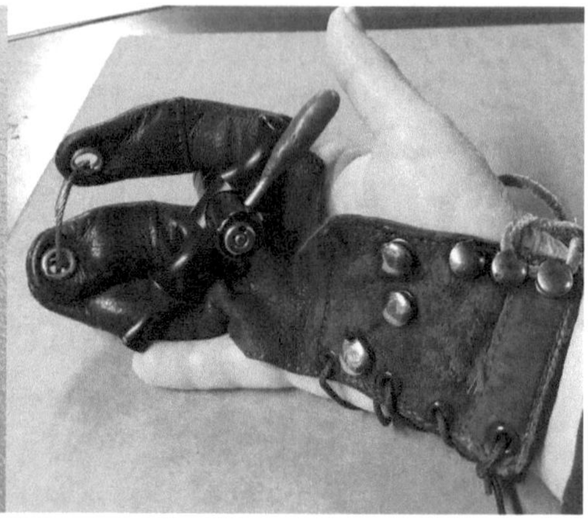

No matter what type of release, it's important to find a solid anchor point that is consistent. Make sure the archer's alignment is good, and that the anchor is in the same place each time. If possible, the anchor point should be directed against bone so it will be more solid. Also make sure the shoulder of the draw arm is set the same with every shot. If the archer is not able to feel their shoulder, they may be able to use the scapula as a reference. If the archer still has an arm, but it is not useable (for example, after a stroke), it may be best to secure the arm against the body.

With all the suggestions so far, the modifications have been to the release or the way it is held and activated; no modifications have been made to the bow or the way it is held. Some archers choose to hold the bow and modify the release, others may choose to hold the release and modify the way the bow is held. The bow can be held with bandages or with a gripping glove (sometimes called a quad glove, see *next photos*). A gripping glove goes around the hand, putting it into a gripping position. The gripping glove shown is by Active Hands (see *info below*). The bow goes into the hand and then is held on by a strap that pulls the fingers around the bow and holds them there. The bow can also be attached to a prosthesis as long as it is not a rigid connection and the bow can move after the arrow release.

The bow glove and the release glove are similar, but the release glove is often less bulky. Once the archer is strapped in, the coach needs to remember the athlete will most likely not be very mobile.

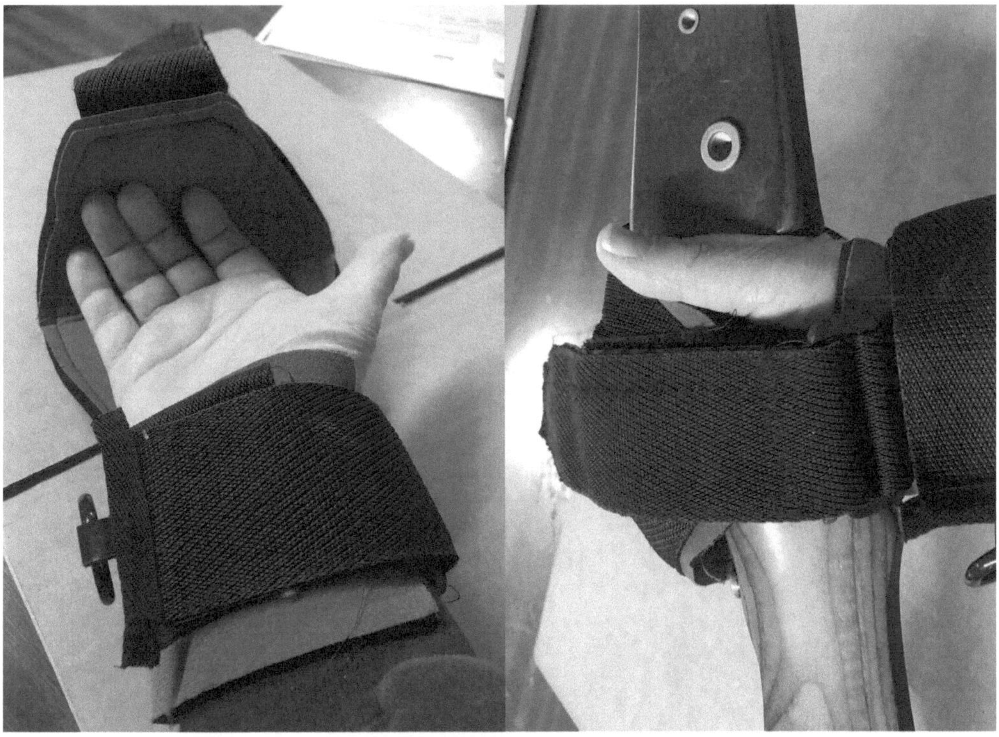

You may need to work at finding ways to make it easier to scope the arrows and possibly to get sips of water.

Most archers are now familiar with Matt Stutzman, the "Armless Archer." Matt was born without arms and taught himself to shoot using his feet. He has a strap that goes around his chest and holds his release. He uses his feet to hold the bow and to hold the bow up to his release to load the arrows. He then draws by pushing his leg out and sets off the release by both pushing and pulling. Neither his bow nor his release have been adapted; the only equipment adaptation is the strap to hold his release. Matt also has a video in the Adaptive Sports Series put together by Disabled Sports USA and USA Archery (https://www.youtube.com/watch?v=Kf15h3hlHwU&list=PLK7QwuzL25xm8yOglKjbFlc2Rt0whPpSw&index=11). Some archers who shoot with their feet use releases very similar to the release Keith uses.

When adapting for archers, be sure to be creative and focus on what will work instead of what won't. If you have an idea and you're not sure how to make it work, check with an occupational therapist or a prosthetic expert. They are usually very willing to help.

For competition, all the above modifications are allowed, but if shooting in para-archery categories make sure any adaptations are included on the classification form (more information in a later chapter). There are some restrictions on strapping and in most competitions, nothing electronic is allowed.

References

• ***Active Hands*** activehands.com Gripping aids that hold the hands in a gripping shape. They also have many other adaptive aids.

• ***Fabtech Systems*** fabtechsystems.com Prosthetic components; have helped with shoulder releases

• ***Adaptive Sports Manual***
https://www.disabledsportsusa.org/sport/archery/

• ***GX4 Adaptive Archery*** https://gx4adaptivearchery.com

Chapter 11
Lower Body Adaptations

Having an impairment in the lower body usually affects the archer, not the equipment. Some archers will need to use stools, some use wheelchairs, and some may have something adapted for them that goes under one leg to make both legs even.

Stability and balance are usually the biggest issues for archers who shoot from a standing position but have some sort of dysfunction in one or both of their legs. The goal is to have the feet positioned so they are stable, and ideally, have the hips and shoulders level as well.

If one leg is shorter than the other, the archer can use either a board under the shorter leg, or have the shoe built up. For Timmy "Doorstop" Palumbo, a doorstop is the perfect solution. Michael Lukow sometimes uses a board under his foot. These are both simple adaptations, and for both archers, no other adaptations are necessary (*see next photo*).

A table saw support stand can be used to help brace someone with balance issues who prefers to shoot from a standing position. It's taller than most stools, and the archer can stand against it rather than sitting on it. The height can also be adjusted and for comfort, a "swim noodle" can be cut and attached.

Archers who have a prosthetic leg might have issues with balance, especially on uneven, wet, or muddy ground. It's worth trying different shoes or a different stance to see if they can take care of the issues. The stance may be non-typical, but balance and stability are most important. The coach can observe posture in all directions and make sure the archer's weight is evenly distributed on both legs. This is sometimes easiest to see by checking that the hips are level. Most archers who have two prosthetic legs will choose to sit on a stool or use a wheelchair. If they do choose to stand, pay attention to the same things. (If they are going to compete, it may be worth encouraging them to shoot from a stool or wheelchair. The rules do not allow them to switch back and forth from standing to sitting, and sitting will be more secure in adverse weather.)

Occasionally archers who use stools or bracing also need upper body adaptations. The upper body will work more efficiently if the lower body is stable and secure, so be sure to pay attention to both.

For archers who need to sit, but don't use wheelchairs, there are several options. Drummer's thrones are one of the more popular options because they are height adjustable and usually will come apart so they can be packed. Some archers construct custom seats that are light weight and easy to pack. Ideally, archers should be able to have both feet securely on the ground.

It's best if stools and stands can be secured in place. Outdoors on dirt and grass, they can often be staked, but more outdoor tournaments now have the shooting line on a hard surface, such as a track or a built-up platform. Anti-slip material on the bottom of the stand or on the legs of the chair can help. Some venues may allow the stand to be secured with duct tape or sandbags or something similar. An archer can stand on the base of their stand, but this might affect their posture.

Wheelchairs

When an archer who is using a wheelchair is starting out, the most important things to watch for are that the archer is stable and that parts of the chair are not in the way, for example armrests. Armrests can often be moved out of the way, and swim noodles or pillows can be used to stabilize the archer if necessary. Make sure the bow is not resting on the wheel or arm rest before release; it will cause the arrow to go high.

There are modifications that can be made to wheelchairs to make them better for shooting.

Better Cushion Cushions come in different thicknesses and can be made of different materials. Some of the materials are not as firm as others. Some can be molded to better fit the athlete. It's important to find one that fits, but it also must allow for some weight re-distribution and/or repositioning in order to avoid pressure sores. Some archers choose to have a cushion specifically for archery; one that might be a little more firm. However, they can also use their everyday cushion.

More Dump Dump is the angle of the seat from the front to the back. Adjusting the dump can change the athlete's center of gravity and improve balance. We've found that the dump that is best for archery is usually pretty good for day to day getting around as well. In most newer wheelchairs it's easy to adjust, so you can try different angles. On a lot of wheelchairs, the wheels can be moved forwards and backwards as well. In the next photo if you look at the way both Andre and Ben are sitting you can see that the front of the seat is slightly higher than the back of the seat.)

Extra Wheel Sometimes the push rim on the bow arm side of the wheelchair will get in the way of the bowstring. Archers can have a wheel without a push rim that is used only for archery. Wheels on wheelchairs are usually easy to take off and put on, so it's an easy adjustment

Holder for Spotting Scope For archers using wheelchairs who can't lean over easily, there are adaptations that can be made for holding scopes. One option is to use a Manfrotto *Magic Arm* (an arm used for photographer's lights). The arm can be clamped onto the wheelchair and the scope can be attached to the arm and moved in and out as necessary (*see next photo*). The Manfrotto *Magic Arm* (*left in the photo*) can be clamped to the wheelchair and moved around. The photo on the right shows how the scope is attached. The quiver has an attachment on it that slides into a clamp on the other side of the wheelchair.

Ben attaches his spotting scope to a swing away arm but he has a strap around his chest so he is unable to lean over to look through it. He has put his phone camera on his spotting scope so that he can see the target on the screen of his phone. He put a tube around it to shade it from the glare of the sun (*see last photos*). Note—This can be used for practice, but is no longer legal for competition.

Several interesting methods of attaching quivers have also been figured out by archers. Some use the bracket and clamp described above; some have come up with a way to put the quiver on the ground; and others may put it between their legs. Be creative and come up with something that works!

Chapter 12
Severe and Multiple Disabilities

You may have the opportunity to work with individuals who have severe disabilities and/or multiple disabilities. Sometimes they can be the most challenging archers to work with, but they can also be the most rewarding.

While working with more severely disabled archers, it is important to make sure that they are taking part in the execution of the shot. You might be doing most of the work, but they might be able to guide the bow to aim, or they might be able to hold a string or release aid along with you and help with the release.

An important safety issue to always keep in mind is to pay attention to what the followthrough will be. Make sure the bow won't hit anyone or anything after the arrow leaves and make sure you know what will happen when the release is activated. (We had a young boy shooting with us who had fairly severe cerebral palsy. After several successful shots where he got assistance with the release, he wanted to try to do it himself. When he let the string go, his hand came back and hit him in the face. Archery wasn't much fun after that.) You also need to make sure the archer can regain their balance and that the chair or wheelchair (if they are using one) is stable and secure.

Some Ideas

Note—always remember to shoot at a close target with light bows! It's a lot more fun when you can hit the target!

- Use large targets—a 122 cm target at 10-15 meters can be lots of fun and easy to hit. For some, you might want to go even closer.
- Throw some of the conventional ideas out: archers don't need to stand perpendicular to the target; facing it may work better. The bow can be held horizontally instead of vertically. Arrow rests that prevent arrows falling off, like a Whisker Biscuit, which are usually used on compound bows, can be used on recurve bows.
- You can strap the bow onto the bow hand and you can strap a release onto the string hand. You can use elastic bandages or grip-

ping gloves. This can give the archer some support so they can help with more of the shot (see *next photos*).

- Mechanical releases can be used with any bows; you can come up

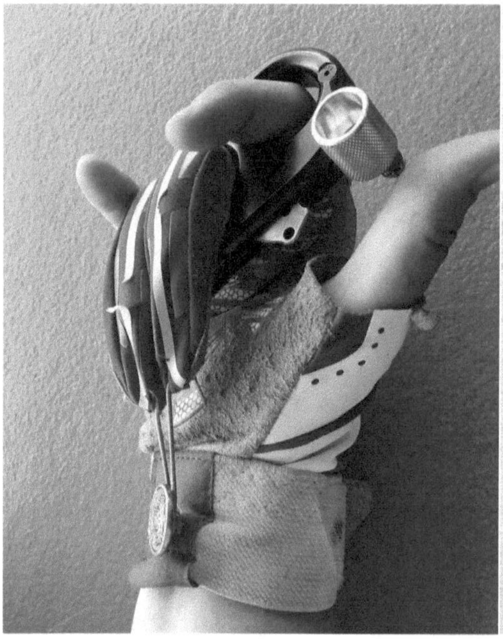

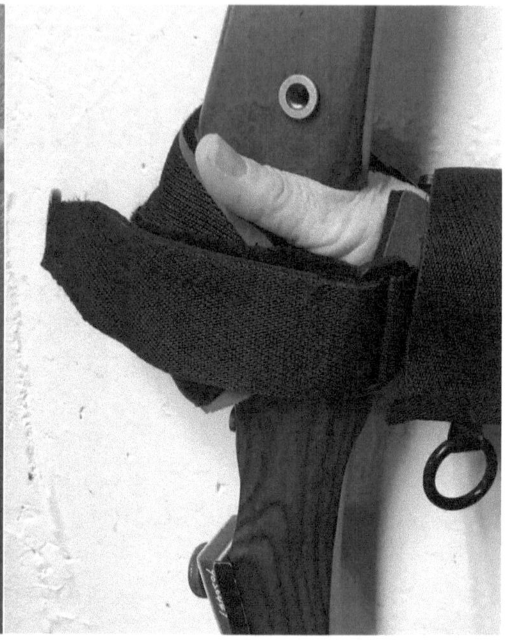

with different ways of releasing them. You can secure the release and hook a string to the release, then hook the string to a body part the archer can control. The archer can touch the release to their face – or they can pull it back and when ready someone else can set off the release.
- Use a bow stand that holds the bow (see *next photos*). An assistant can help with drawing the string back and aiming. Wheelchairs and chairs can be placed in several different positions to find what works best. You might be able to hook a release to a power wheelchair, the archer can back up, using the power of the chair to draw the bow, then get sighting assistance if necessary, and when ready release the arrow.
- You can place yourself behind the archer and assist them with both holding the bow and the string and possibly aiming. Your hand can be over their hand (be sure not to hold too tightly). You and the archer can aim and then count to three; on three, you both release the string (see last photo).
- If you have an archer who can pull back but sometimes pulls too far, you can tie a string from the grip of the bow to the nocking point on the bow string. The string you tie will restrict how far the bow can be drawn.

believe

Resources

• ***Active Hands*** activehands.com Gripping aids that hold the hands in a gripping shape. They also have many other adaptive aids.

• ***Archery Shooter Systems*** www.bowhanger.com Maker of many kinds of bow stands, look under "NASP Approved" or "Indoor Hangers" for Archer Assist Stand.

Chapter 13
Adaptations for Archers with Visual Impairments

People who have visual impairments can and do shoot archery! Depending on the distance and the target, some archers will not need any adaptations. For others, the adaptations can be simple, such as having something to tell them where to stand and someone to spot for them; others have customized foot locators and tactile sights.

Before starting to shoot, introduce the archer to the equipment. Let them hold the bow and the arrow and explain how they go together. Be sure to explain all of the parts: handle, limbs, string, nocking point, arrow rest, etc. Explain the safety rules and how they work. If you have another archer nearby who is willing, have them hold the bow (the one you are demonstrating with) and let the new archer feel the hook on the string hand and the grip on the bow hand. The demonstrating archer can then go to full draw and let the new archer feel the shoulders and hands. (Not all archers are willing to be a demonstrator like this; be sure to ask privately ahead of time.) If you don't have an archer who will demonstrate, you can explain it and help the archer get into proper position: first without a bow, and then with a bow. (Stretch bands can help with this.)

You can practice the entire sequence including the release and followthrough with a stretch band. If the archer is using a release aid, you can put a D-loop on the stretch band. This process sounds like it will take a long time, but it can be done fairly quickly. After the first shots, be sure to ask if there are any questions and make sure the archer understands the process.

While the archer is trying out archery, you can use something simple to help them know where to stand and which way they should be facing. However, it does need to be something heavy enough that it won't move or something that can be secured. It also helps if it can orient the archer to the target. It could be a block of wood taped to the floor or a chair. A fairly simple foot locator can be made from

PVC pipe (*see photos below*).

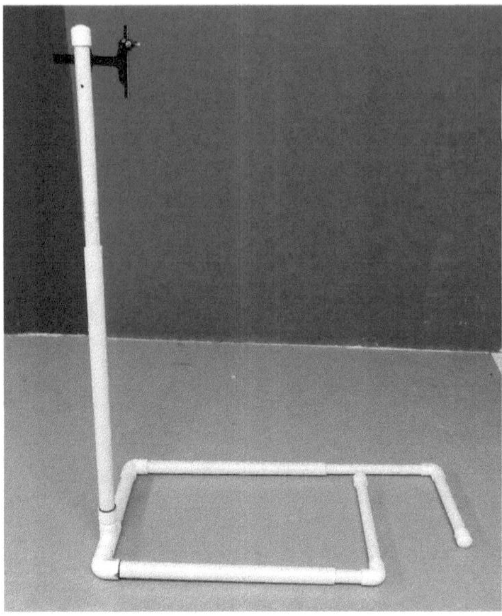

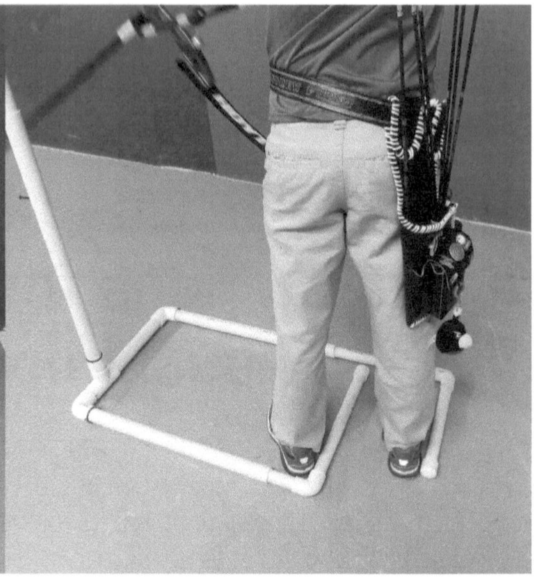

Put the arrows in a quiver which is close enough so the archer can reach them without moving their feet. Help the archer get the proper stance and if necessary, load the arrow onto the bow. Help when necessary, but let the archer do as much as possible independently. Assist the archer to draw the bow and achieve anchor, and then stand behind them and help them aim.

A tactile sight enables the archer to "aim" by placing the back of their hand against a protrusion. A lot of VI archers are able to use a tactile sight during their first session. Of course you would introduce and explain it while you were explaining how it all works. The tactile

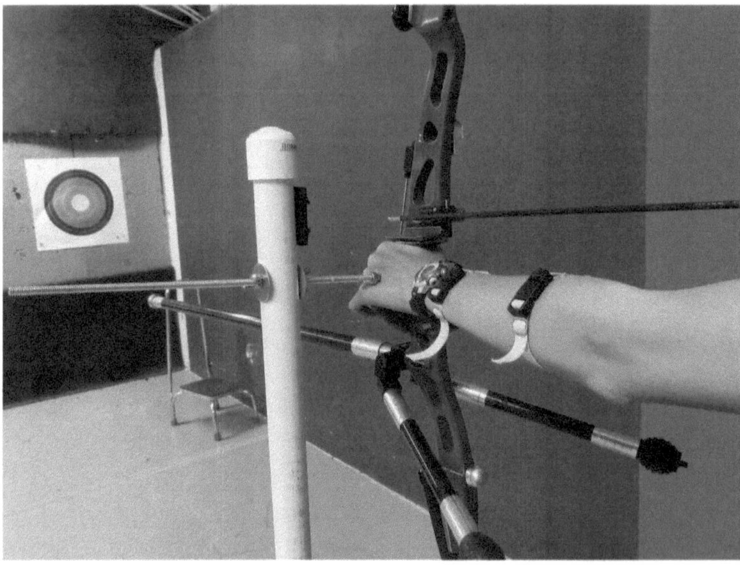

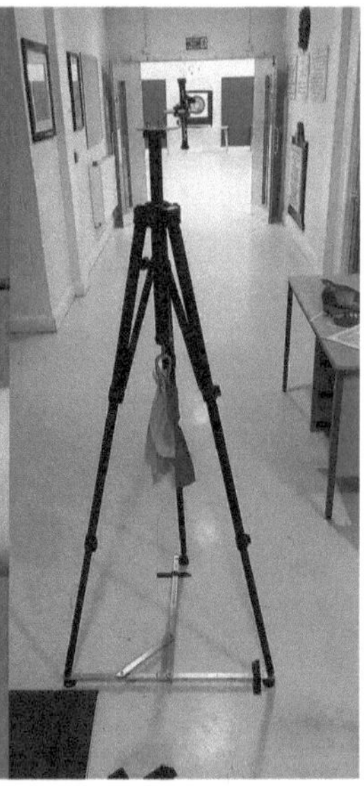

sight is often connected to (or part of) the foot locator. (Information on more permanent stands and regulations for competition are included in a later chapter.) You can also put a sight on a tripod (see *photos above*).

After the archer finishes shooting their arrows, they can walk down to the target with you. They can stand to the side while you explain where their arrows are. The easiest way is often by using a clock face; for example, there is an arrow in the nine ring at 2:00 o'clock and one in the seven ring at 5:00 o'clock. Make sure the archer understands the clock face; we get archers quite often who have only seen digital clocks! Walk back to the shooting line and repeat.

There are a few things you can do to make it easier for a visually impaired archer to shoot independently.

- Put together a tactile sight. This is a sight placed at the height of the bow hand at full draw. This can be done by taping a sight to a tripod.
- Instead of looking at the sight, the archer puts it against their hand.
- Put a rope at waist height from the waiting line to the side of the target. Tie a knot (large enough to feel) where the rope intersects the shooting line. Tie a second knot that lets the archer know they are getting close to the target. Tie a third knot close enough to the target for the archer to pull their arrows, but make it far enough away that they don't make contact with the arrows. You'll also want to tie a knot the archer can use after retrieving the arrows to know where the shooting line is.
- Glue string on the lines of the target so the archer can feel them and can feel where their arrows are located before pulling them.

Resources

There are a lot of good videos on YouTube. Look up visually impaired archery. Here are some links:

- World Archery: https://www.youtube.com/watch?v=TcvM3zdBhal

- https://www.youtube.com/watch?v=DAcO1b0Nh60

- World Archery:
https://www.youtube.com/watch?v=_JYUbYpDopU

- USA Archery: https://www.youtube.com/watch?v=RiiqASwiwSk

Note—The shooting stand shown in the last chapter comes with an adapter so it can be made into a stand for a visually impaired archer.

Janice's Story

by Janice Walth

Picture in your mind a person who has lost their sight, a blind person, what things do you visualize? Someone navigating through a crowded room using a white cane? A person striding down the sidewalk with a beautiful guide dog? Maybe someone kicking back with a Braille book open on their lap or sitting in front of a computer, listening intently to their screen reader? Chances are you don't picture them on a shooting line, pulling back a cool looking bow and hitting a target 30 meters away. No, that image goes more with Robin Hood or Katniss Everdeen. At least you'd have to be able to see the target, right? But I'm here to tell you that it's not true, a person who is blind can shoot a bow and arrow and hit a target. It's not about sight, it's about form, performing the shot correctly.

I'm blind and I've been shooting archery for 18 years. Initially, I just wanted to know what it was like to pull back the bow, shoot the arrow, and hear it hit something. My husband, Courtney, had been shooting for several years with a local club and I guess I was getting kind of tired of sitting on the sidelines. I did some internet searches looking for anyone who was blind and was shooting archery. I wanted to know what kind of technique people who were blind might be using. At that time, I could only find the British Blind Sport organization over in Great Britain. I emailed them and they sent us pictures of the adaptive equipment they had been using. Their archers were even competing in tournaments! Well, that was all it took. Courtney built the foot-locator and tactile sight and I began shooting.

This is how the sighting equipment works. The foot-locator enables a visually impaired archer to return to the same position on the shooting line at the beginning of each shooting end. It's placed on the ground relative to the shooting line, so that the archer can back up against it, touching the back of her heels to it at the position of the foot markers protruding from it. These foot markers are adjustable depending on the archer's preferred stance. When the archer is standing properly, they will have one foot on either side of the shooting line. A tripod holds the tactile sight. The tactile sight enables the visually impaired archer to aim. When set up, the tripod is indexed into the foot-locator so that they become one unit.

The archer raises the bow and touches the back of her bow hand to a probe that protrudes from the tactile sight. The archer is allowed only this contact point for sighting. A spotter guides the visually impaired archer to the shooting line in the area of the foot-marker. The spotter then stands three feet behind the shooting line, directly behind the archer. This spotter tells the archer where the arrow hits the target after each arrow is shot. The spotter indicates the color of the ring and the position in that ring by saying the clock face, for example: Red, 10 o'clock; Blue, 3 o'clock. After each shooting end, the spotter guides the archer to the target to retrieve arrows and may assist with scoring.

In 2004, I shot at a couple of state-level sanctioned tournaments as a guest, which resulted in the creation of a visually impaired category for California. Courtney and I then decided we'd like to participate in the U.S. Nationals, and that resulted in my being the first blind archer to participate in the U.S. Nationals.

Then, much to my surprise, in 2007 I was asked by head Para coach Randi Smith to accompany the U.S. Paralympic archery team to the World Championships in South Korea. Just imagine, all I wanted to do was try shooting a bow and arrow, and now I was on my way to South Korea to compete internationally! So, after months of fund raising I found myself on the archery field in South Korea with visually impaired archers from Great Britain, France, Belgium and Italy. I'd never competed against anyone but myself before, as here in the States I was the only competitive archer who was visually impaired, but, there I was.

On the first day of qualifiers, we were going to be shooting six arrows in four minutes, and we'd do this six times for the first round. The horn sounded and I shot my first six arrows . . . all misses. Well, I made that easy for them to score, but how embarrassing was that? Now we were ready for the second end. The horn sounded and my first 5 arrows were all misses. I don't even know what that sixth arrow was, I was just so mortified. Eleven misses in a row! But somehow I got my shot together. Imagine my surprise when I found out I was ranked third going into the elimination rounds! Imagine even more incredibly that I actually shot the highest score in the semifinals and wound up in the gold medal match! I won the silver medal, set some world records and came home with a whole lot of great memories.

Two years later, I participated in another World Championship, which took place in the Czech Republic. The experience couldn't have been more different. It was really hard not to have expectations based on how well I'd done two years previous. That was my first mistake. I knew that would be the worst thing I could do to my mental game, but it's not an easy thing to suppress. My second mistake was to increase the poundage of my bow a week before the competition. And the third bad decision was changing my form before the semifinals. In spite of setting two world records during the qualifying round, I was intimidated by the other archers and lost my confidence. I wound up coming in last. But that didn't dampen my enthusiasm for the sport or for my love of competition.

In 2015 I was able to compete in my third World Championships in Germany. I was determined not to crash and burn again and developed a training strategy to prepare for the competition. I told myself that I needed to believe in myself; to believe that I know how to shoot and can do it consistently if I'm focused; to trust my coach and don't question what he tells me; and to train my nervous system to fire my muscles and remember how powerful my muscles can be. I won the gold medal that year and set a new world record. I've continued to compete nationally and internationally and the category is slowly growing.

Archers come from all walks of life, all ages, and all abilities. Entire families participate together. For me, archery is about more than just the participation in a sport. Archery builds confidence, gives me a feeling of accomplishment, and a sense of inclusion. This feeling of inclusion helps a person feel good about them self, and can help cross a threshold that will open up even more possibilities in their lives. I believe archery enables someone who is blind to accomplish something they had not even considered to be possible. The experience directly effects how they feel about themselves, and their own capabilities.

I'm dedicated to exposing as many people as I can to the sport, in the hope that, no matter what challenges they face, they can know what it feels like to work hard and experience the success that comes from it.

Chapter 14
Competion Opportunities

Some athletes like to compete, others do not. For those who do, there are different levels of competition for both youths and adults. Athletes with disabilities are welcome at most tournaments but it's generally better to start at local, state, and regional competitions, where things are a little more relaxed than at national events. At local events officials are usually prepared for first time competitors and have more time to answer questions.

There are also a lot of regional multi-sport, multi-disability events that are good first events. The Endeavor Games and the Move United Junior Nationals are two of the largest. You can find information on those events at www.moveunited.com. The National Veterans' Wheelchair Games also has a large archery tournament and the Veterans' Administration does several other events. The Warrior Games and Invictus Games are competitions for injured soldiers and veterans, but they have specific trials and eligibility requirements that are not the same as the Paralympic Games.

Adult archers who have disabilities do have separate para categories in USA Archery tournaments, but to shoot in those categories, an archer must be classified, either nationally or internationally. If an archer needs a chair or stool (or wheelchair) and they are not classified, they can still shoot in the tournaments, but they won't be in the para categories.

In the USA, youth archers can shoot at most JOAD (Junior Olympic Archery Development, under USA Archery) competitions without being classified. They can use whatever adaptive equipment they need. They don't shoot in a separate category, instead they shoot in their own age group, with other archers shooting the same kind of equipment. Para categories for youth are now being offered at all national USA Archery events, but youth will need to be classified to shoot in those categories.

Other archery organizations in the USA usually don't have separate categories for archers who have disabilities, but they are welcoming and accommodating. Some field and 3-D tournaments may not be physically accessible due to the natural terrain, but the other archers will often assist when necessary.

Resources

- ***The Endeavor Games*** (www.moveunited.com)
- ***The Move United Junior Nationals*** (www.moveunited.com)
- ***The National Veterans' Wheelchair Games*** (https://wheelchairgames.org/)
- ***The Warrior Games*** (https://dodwarriorgames.com)
- ***The Invictus Games*** (https://invictusgamesfoundation.org)

Chapter 15
Competition Classifications

Not all archers who use adaptive equipment or who have disabilities choose to compete. For those who are eligible, and interested in international competition, archery is offered in the Paralympic Games every four years and World Championships are held every two years. Other tournaments at national and international levels are held throughout the world as well.

In para-archery, as in other Paralympic sports, athletes are classified according to their disability and their function. The goal of the classifications is to ensure that athletes are shooting against other athletes with similar abilities.

Archers must have an eligible impairment to be classified. Eligible impairments for archery include impaired muscle power, impaired passive range of motion, loss of limb or limb deficiency, hypertonia, ataxia, and visual impairments. Some non-eligible impairments include pain, joint instability, and impaired endurance. For a complete list and more information, check the World Archery Classification Handbook (https://worldarchery.sport/sport/disciplines/para-archery).

To compete internationally in para-archery, the disabled archer must be internationally classified. Archers need to be either nationally or internationally classified to shoot in the para categories in USA tournaments. (A schedule of events with classification opportunities is on the USA Archery website (www.USArchery.org).) Archers who have disabilities, but who are not classified can still shoot in USA Archery tournaments, but not in the para categories.

In order to be classified, there are medical forms that need to be completed by a doctor and returned to the National Governing Body (USA Archery in the United States, Archery GB in the UK, etc.). National classification can be done in an athlete's own country and the rules for classification are determined by that country. International classification is done at international events and is usually done by two classifiers from countries other than the country the archer is from. If an athlete is classified at an international event and one of the classifiers happens to be from the athlete's country, the classification is usually given a review status and the athlete will need to go through the process again at the next international event.

Classifiers are physical therapists or other professionals who are able to correctly evaluate physical function. The classifiers evaluate the athlete and watch the athlete shoot. They then give the athlete a classification card (or paper) that the athlete keeps. The evaluation process can be painful and exhausting so archers and coaches should keep that in mind when scheduling the classification.

There are six functional (or physical) classifications in Paralympic Archery. (*Important*—These classifications are not the same as the shooting categories.) These are very basic descriptions; more information is available on the World Archery website. The most comprehensive descriptions are in the Classifiers' Handbook.

These six categories are classified by World Archery classifiers:

W1 Archers This is the most severely impaired group. They have some sort of disability that affects at least three limbs and their trunk. They shoot from a wheelchair.

W2 Archers These archers use a wheelchair for mobility but have good hand and arm function. They shoot from a wheelchair with their feet on the wheelchair footrests.

ST Archers ST (standing) archers with a physical disability usually shoot from a standing position. Many of the archers use a stool or some sort of support. They usually have their feet on the ground. Archers who shoot with their feet are usually in this category.

NE (Non-Eligible) Athletes who have a disability and go through the classification process but who don't meet the requirements are classified as Non-Eligible. Sometimes they are given a classification card that shows any adaptive equipment they use. It is not necessary to have this classification to use adaptive equipment and shoot in the non-para classes.

VI 1 and VI 2/3 Combined There are two visually impaired classes. The classification process for archers with visual impairments is different. They have paperwork which is completed by the athlete's ophthalmologist. The paperwork is then sent to the National Governing Body and then to World Archery for final classification. The VI 1 archers use blindfolds; VI 2/3 archers do not need to use blindfolds.

Shooting Classes

There are five shooting classes in Para-Archery. After archers are physically classified, they are put into shooting classes.

W1 Archers Most W1 archers shoot compound bows, but they could choose to shoot recurve bows. If they shoot in the W1 class, they are limited to 45 pounds with no levels, peeps, or magnification. If there are enough archers, men and women are separated, but they can also be combined. An archer classified as W1 could choose to shoot in the Open category (*see next photos*).

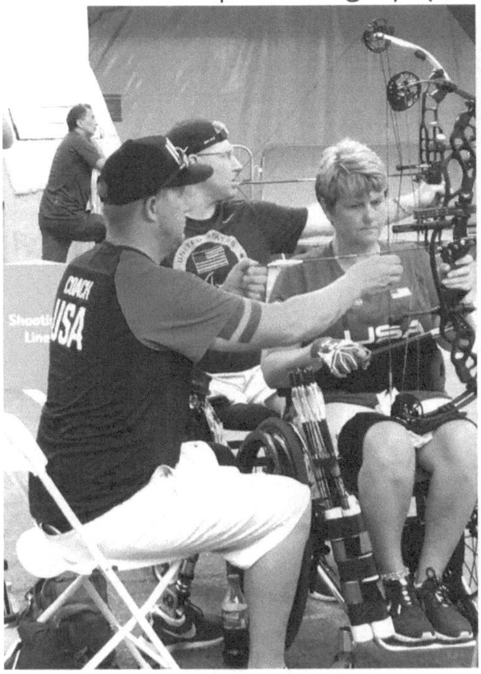

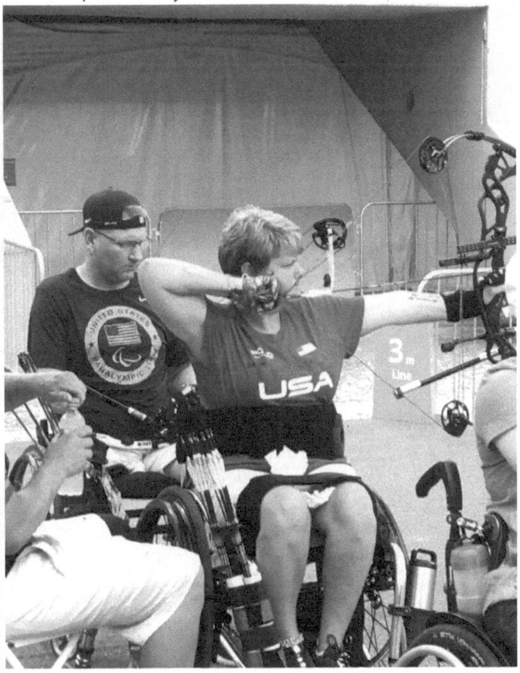

Open Recurve W2 and ST archers who shoot recurve bows are combined into the open recurve class. W1 archers can choose to shoot in this class as well. Men and women are separated. The rules are World Archery recurve rules (*see next photo* — all three are ST

archers shooting recurves)

Open Compound W2 and ST archers who shoot compound bows are combined into the open compound class. W1 archers can also choose this class if they want to shoot by regular World Archery compound rules. Men and women are separated. The rules are World Archery compound rules (see *next photo*)

VI 1 archers use blindfolds; VI 2/3 do not. Men and women are combined, and they can shoot either recurve or compound bows. If there are not enough visually impaired archers at an event, the VI 1 and VI 2/3 classes can be combined, and all archers wear blindfolds. All archers are limited to a 45-pound draw weight.

In national and international tournaments, the stand can be set up at the beginning of the event and left there until the end. VI 1 archers must be blindfolded at all times on the FOP.

Chapter 16
Tournaments

Archers with disabilities often need to do a little more planning to participate in tournaments. Coaches can help with this, and they can also help the organizers plan for the archers.

Tournament Preparation – For The Archer

Getting from the parking lot to the shooting area can be the first challenge. Figuring out a way to get their bow case and everything else from here to there takes some creativity. Some archers use carrier hooks on the front of their wheelchair that the case can sit on. Others hook the bow case to the back of the chair with climbing carabineers (the bow case needs to have wheels to do this). Putting everything into a wagon is another option for some. There are generally people willing to help, but archers should plan ahead or bring a friend to assist in case no one is available.

Archers who use wheelchairs or stools often stay on the shooting line (especially during outdoor events) between ends rather than going back and forth, so planning ahead for that is also important.

These are some things that archers and coaches need to think about.

Weather Weather happens at every tournament, so it is an important thing to consider. Archers should have an umbrella to protect them from both the sun and the rain. Sunscreen is important also, and is often easiest if applied at home. Appropriate clothing needs to be considered, again remembering they might be staying on the line while others head underneath tents.

Layering is the best idea, with clothes for staying dry on the list. In an emergency, large garbage bags work to keep an archer dry, but planning ahead and having appropriate clothes is better. Many archers will choose to not use rain gear because it's bulky and/or difficult to get on (this makes the umbrella even more important!) If this is the case, they should have dry clothes they can change into or put on after they are finished shooting. Remember also, that for archers in wheelchairs, it is important to think about keeping the lap and the wheelchair cushion dry when possible. Large garbage bags can be used to keep equipment and backpacks dry.

Archers who have issues with temperature regulation will have problems with heat and cold and these can be magnified if they are also wet. Cooling vests are available (but can be expensive and bulky), but spray bottles and cool towels on the neck and head can also work. Metal water bottles can be filled with hot water or ice water depending on what is needed, but care must be taken that the archer does not get burned by the bottle (cold and hot can both burn). Putting ice in a hat and then placing the hat on the head can be unpleasant for some, but for others it works well.

Nutrition Hydration and snacks before, during, and after the tournament are important also. A small cooler that the archer can keep near them at the shooting line works well. A water bottle that can easily be refilled is important; other archers will generally help with the refilling. Snacks need to be easy to eat, not messy or sticky, and they need to not cause bathroom issues. It's a good idea to try new snacks at home days before the competition.

Restrooms Bathrooms at tournaments can be a major issue. Not only is it often an adventure to get to them; once there, the archer with a disability may not be able to get into them. This can then cause other issues, because if the archer knows the bathroom is inaccessible, eating and drinking may be avoided. This can then cause dehydration and other medical issues.

Other Archers should also try to anticipate other needs. Music or books can be nice diversions between ends. Both a wet towel and a dry towel are handy to have. Other recommended items include a small notebook and pen, an arrow puller (for people who are pulling), arrow lube, and any necessary tools that could be needed for minor sight or bow adjustments.

Tournament Etiquette

Because archers with disabilities often depend on others to help out, it's very important that they are courteous and prepared. Even though other archers will usually help, the athlete needs to realize that others are not obligated to help. Therefore, whenever possible, the archer should plan on bringing his or her own agent to help with scoring and pulling arrows. If that is not possible, the archer should contact the Tournament Director (TD) and let the TD know that an agent will be needed. Most TDs and tournament organizers are happy to help in any way they can, but many small tournaments don't have a lot of extra people available. (USA Archery's policy is that archers are responsible for providing their own agents and agents must have background checks and passed SafeSport.)

When agents are not available, it is okay to ask one of the other archers on the target to pull and score the arrows; but again, that person is under no obligation to do so. If they do agree to pull, the disabled archer needs to make sure that, if necessary, the arrows are adequately and frequently lubed.

Archers using wheelchairs or stools or other adaptive aids, need to stay within their own space. They need to be aware of what and who is in front of and behind them so they don't run over anything or anyone. At the end of the tournament, the archer needs to be sure to thank the agent and let the agent know the help was appreciated.

Tournament Preparation – For The Tournament Director

Field Set Up There are some things that will be important for disabled archers no matter what the event. These would include things such as restrooms, parking, weather protection, and hydration. Making sure these things are available for the archer with a disability means that everyone will be able to use them.

Restrooms Restrooms should be accessible – and the archers need to be able to get to them. Accessible bathrooms that are up a flight of a stairs, or on the other side of the field, are not a good option. It is nice, when possible, to have a family restroom for archers who may need assistance. Wheelchair accessible portable restrooms can be rented.

Parking Parking should also be close if possible, and there should be ramps or good access from the parking to the field. If parking isn't close, having someone available to help carry gear and/or push wheelchairs to the field is another option. Gravel, loose sand, and muddy parking lots are difficult to navigate in a wheelchair, as are cobblestones and potholes. Hills, uneven terrain, and long or wet grass are also difficult.

Field Access Barriers between the shooter area and spectator area can occasionally be a safety issue. If there is an emergency, make sure the athletes can get quickly off the field. At a tournament I was at recently, access to the shooting area was very limited so athletes had to go quite a distance to get from the access point to their shooting spot. As a general rule, that might not be a big issue, but in case of an emergency, it could be a huge issue. It's a good idea to make sure one person (either field crew or tournament staff) is appointed to make sure that in an emergency, all archers who need help are in a safe location.

Weather Weather protection includes protection from the sun as well as from the rain. It might be on the shooting line, or it might be nearby where the athletes can easily get to it. It could be portable

shade tents or it might be a permanent structure near the shooting field. Most of the time, the athletes will bring their own individual protection (rain gear, umbrellas, etc.). In areas where extreme weather (lightning, tornadoes, etc) is likely, be sure to take the archers who have disabilities into consideration when planning emergency procedures. Artificial turf can get very hot which is not a good thing for archers with temperature issues or for amputees with lower leg prostheses or braces; the elevated temperature tends to heat up the prosthesis or brace and can burn the arm or leg.

Nutrition and Hydration Hydration options need to be available and easy to access. Sometimes refillable water bottles are the easiest option, but someone may need to be available to refill them for the archers. If snack bars or concessions are available, make sure archers who have disabilities can get to them.

Awards Awards are important to archers and being able to get on the podium is part of that experience. Either have an award stand that everyone can get on or don't use one at all. Some competitions have used stakes in the ground, labeled 1st, 2nd, and 3rd, and the archers stand/sit behind them.

Russell's Story

by Russell Wolfe

I hope this covers a few things like how I started in archery, how it became more than a sport and my biggest highlights.

So, how did it begin? I started as most do, shooting in my backyard with my brothers. Growing up in the country there really wasn't much to do. Shooting in the yard eventually turned into chasing game in the woods. Life eventually happened and I graduated high school and joined the military. Ten years later I was involved in an accident and broke my back. Congratulations . . . and welcome to the world of being paralyzed. Of course, this new life without use of my legs created a world of loneliness and depression. Two years after being paralyzed I was invited to the Veteran Wheelchair Games. I saw two sports on the registration packet that interested me, archery and air gun. Let's say this was the start.

I consider myself an introvert at heart and in my opinion, this is ideal for archery. I am a self-motivator so it was/is easy for me to set a goal and go after it. My training got a boost about two years into shooting when my relationship at the time, during an argument, informed me that she didn't know why I did archery because I had no "natural talent." My opinion was, okay, you say I have no natural talent, that just means I will have to work harder than anyone else. After all "hard work beats talent, when talent doesn't work hard."

I decided in 2004 that I wanted to go to the Paralympics in 2008. I got a coach and their first impression was, it was possible to make that event but not probable. Okay, another challenge. Challenge accepted.

I made my first national team in 2006 or 2007 as a Recurve archer. This, I thought, was the greatest accomplishment in archery for me. The score I shot to make the team ranked 15th in the world and hence qualified me for the 2008 Paralympics. Okay, another milestone, as I had made the goal of making it to the Paralympics. The experience at the 2008 Paralympics left me reeling. My performance was not stellar and I was embarrassed. This lit another fire under me

and I decided I could not quit now without redeeming myself. I set my sights on the 2009 World Championships but with a different goal. My goal at this tournament was to shoot my shot and not worry about the results.

During the 2009 World Championships it was hot. I mean it was people dropping on the line hot. I had been training in 90+ degree heat and 90%+ humidity so I was able to handle the heat and I stuck to my plan of shooting my form. After qualifications I believe I was in 11th position. It was my highest standing at a World Championship to date. My score was not necessarily the greatest because of the way it lined me up in the eliminations. Either way I decided to shoot my shot and just be happy with whatever happened. I went through the first elimination round and won. I went to the second elimination against an archer ranked higher than me and I won again. I remember this was against a Polish archer because he had beaten me for a Gold medal at an earlier competition at Stoke Mandeville in England. I not only beat this archer but I beat him convincingly. Off to the matches to decide who goes for a Gold Medal. Great, I get put up against a Korean archer who has been competing for 22 years as a para-archer, while I have been doing this for three or four years with a recurve bow.

Let the games begin! Three arrow ends and total score will take the match. We started off with matching scoring arrows and then the match went back and forth with him leading then I would lead. In the end he won the match by one point! Here is where one of my proudest moments in my archery career came from. The entire Korean team lined up and shook my hand for a hard-fought match. I had earned the respect of the Korean team. Anyone who knows archery will know that this is unheard of. I had never seen this happen before and have never seen it since.

I went on to win the Bronze at the 2009 Para World Championships. That win was, in my research, the first individual medal in Para Archery Recurve for the USA since the early 70's. I went on to make another Paralympic team, to London in 2012. I finished tied for 9th in London.

I discovered in 2013 that I had two labrum tears in my left shoulder due to a hand-cycling accident. I remember before the accident that my scores were climbing like never before. After the accident I could barely raise my bow and shooting was a chore and painful. I am not sure if I will ever get back to where I was, but I know that archery was the factor that kept me going through many a day.

There are so many stories I could share about my archery. Instead let me share this: no matter who you are or what you believe in, take your shot, and believe in you.

Chapter 17
My Coaching Tips

I've learned a lot about myself and my coaching over the years. These are some tips, which basically are skills that all coaches need that nobody teaches or that you learn in the school of hard knocks

1. Know your own coaching philosophy. Find your own style and get comfortable with it.

Some coaches are loud and "in your face." Others are quiet and better in the background. Find what works for you and what you are comfortable with. Athletes are pretty good at adapting if they know you're being genuine. If they don't like your style, maybe one of the other coaches on your team will be a better fit.

Figure out what is important to you. There are lots of books and articles to help you. Is it more important that you have a group that supports each other or a group that wins? Of course, it's entirely possible to have both, but occasionally they may conflict. Is school more important than archery? Are you okay with athletes missing practice for a family reunion or school play?

2. Know who you are teaching and why.
In this case, you're teaching archery, but you're going to teach kids at a birthday party differently from how you will teach a scout group working on a merit badge. You'll teach the scouts differently from how you'll teach a young adult who wants to go bowhunting. You'll teach Olympic hopefuls differently from how you'll teach a group of date-night college students. You'll also teach differently if you are going to see the students over an extended period rather than just once. It's important to know your audience before you start.

For kids at a birthday party or similar one time event, safety and fun are the most important (in that order). You want to have the kids leave wanting to come back. If and when they come back for lessons, form will become more important, but safety and fun are also still important. At that point, you can determine what their goals are, and where you will go from there. Not all archers want to compete, some may be wanting to hunt and some may want to have an activity to do with their family or friends.

Archers may come into your program who have been shooting on their own or with another coach. You will have to decide where to start. It helps if you know what you think are the most important parts of the shot. It's important that you watch the shot they came in with long enough to really see it. I explain to new archers the first time they come in to my class that I will be mostly watching and they shouldn't be concerned if I don't give them lots of input during that session. After the session we can talk about what they want to do with their archery.

3. The relationship is the most important part.
Not all kids (and adults) are going to be great archers, but they all deserve respect and attention. Get to know the archers. Listen to them and connect. The most important part of a coach-athlete relationship is the relationship. Talk to everyone, every session, and use names. Sometimes this isn't as easy as it sounds, but it makes a difference.

Learning to listen and to hear what the student is "really" saying is important. Pay attention to body language and what they might not be saying. It's okay to ask lots of questions and to clarify anything that isn't clear. Take the time to learn some listening skills and practice them. Many archers won't remember all that you taught them, but they will remember you.

How to give feedback (both positive and negative) is an important part of communicating and can help or hurt a relationship. Think about the "W's when you give feedback: Why (teaching, evaluating, advising)?; Where (on the field, in the office?); When (is it scheduled or spontaneous?); Who (is it a coach or an athlete; one person or a team?).

4. Know what you do and don't know.

It's impossible to know everything about archery (although some people think they do!). You may be an expert at tuning recurve bows, for example, but you might need to get help for a compound bow. You might know the rules for World Archery tournaments, but do you know them for NFAA tournaments? Can you teach an archer to string walk, or do you need to go figure it out? Can you teach an archer to shoot with a mouth tab or do you need to find someone who can? It's okay to ask questions; it's okay to ask for help; and it's okay to say you don't know, but you do need to try to find out. You and your athletes can look for answers together, or depending on the archers, you can challenge them to find out and let you know.

Having a group or a couple of other coaches/athletes/mentors you can go to when you aren't sure of the answer can be very valuable. It might not always be an archery issue, it could be helping an archer find financial support or advice on how to write a resume.

Be sure you know the rules of the game. There are several different types of archery (indoor, 3-D, field, etc.) and within each of them, different organizations (NFAA, USAA, ASA) have their own variations of the rules. When possible, find the rules before you need them; it's better for you and the athlete to be prepared. Within para archery, if an athlete is going to be competitive, they need to know the classification and equipment rules. If you have athletes looking toward higher level competitions, be sure that both you and the athlete (and parents when appropriate) know the anti-doping rules and where to get more information.

5. Make parents part of your team.

In some ways, this has changed a lot since I started coaching. When I started, parents would drop their kids off and come back when class was over. Now they stick around and watch. At first, it seemed like they were watching every move their child made and every move the coach made. Most of them eventually brought books, or knitting, or played on their phones. Having someplace comfortable for them to sit and watch can make things easier for both of you. We have a bench that parents need to stay behind (to avoid confusion), but

where they can easily see how their kids are doing and the kids are able to go back to them.

Remember to communicate with parents. Let them know your philosophy and what you expect from them and from their kids. Make sure they understand what your role is at a competition and what their role is. They are your allies, not your enemies.

It's good to keep parents involved. Let them know how your program runs and what (if anything) you expect of them. If I give younger kids homework, I'll let the parents know what it is and what the purpose is. I have older kids explain it to their parents.

Of course parents can help out at concession stands, tournament registration, and similar things, but they're more willing to do it if you talk to them more often than just when you ask them to help out!

6. Be willing to adapt and learn from others and share your knowledge. Not all archers who come in will be able to shoot using conventional methods. Accommodating them might be as simple as a chair to sit on or finding a different way to hold the bow. Ask questions and make the adapting a partnership, something you are working on together.

Know how to teach and be able to say the same things several different ways (louder doesn't work!). Knowing the steps of a good shot is one thing, knowing how to teach them is quite another thing. You can show an archer a good followthrough so they know what to do, but can you teach them how to do it? Different archers will learn differently and what "clicks" for one, may not work at all for the next one. There are now several "how to shoot archery" videos on the internet and a few of them are pretty good. You can also find other coaches and share information with them.

There isn't just one way to do anything or, said differently, there is more than one way to do everything. Being willing to adapt to the situation, rather than waiting for it to adapt to you, will often get quicker and better results. Training your athletes to be adaptable and able to adjust to different situations (clocks breaking, weather changes, etc.), will pay off in the long run.

As you gain more experience, other coaches may come to you for more information. Be sure to treat them like you'd want to be treated. You can also share what you've learned by teaching instructor courses and helping with community events.

7. Help athletes be responsible for their own performances.

Athletes need to know how to be responsible for their own performances. Some coaches assume that their athletes will pick this up on their own, but especially when starting out, they need some guidance. Help them learn to set up and take down their own equipment, how to adjust their sight, how to recover from a bad shot. When they are ready, teach them to fletch their own arrows and to tune their own bow. Knowing that they can handle most stuff even if the coach or parents aren't there, will help their confidence.

As they get more advanced, they'll need to learn how to spot their own arrows and how to adjust for the wind. They'll need to know how to shoot head to head matches and how team rounds work. These can be a challenge to train for, especially if you have a small group. You can modify the event, keeping the important parts intact or use videos of competitions.

8. Know when to take things personally and when to shake it off or walk away.

Realize you aren't the perfect coach for everyone and archers do change coaches. There are many reasons that archers change coaches and most of them are probably not because of you. They might change because they moved away; they might change because their friends are in a different club; they might change because their goals or priorities changed. It's important to realize that archers will change coaches, and maybe your goal should be to not be their last coach! Try not to take it too personally, and be sure to not bad mouth other coaches, the athletes, or the parents.

Be aware that you may have to deal with the sport's politics and bunk and drivel and know that they are part of the game, and you need to be able to tell them apart! This gets more and more relevant the higher up the ladder you (and sometimes the athlete) goes. It helps to know why you are doing what you are doing, and what your own values are. Along those same lines, if you know your values and why you are coaching, it can make it easier to decide what is worth fighting for, and what is not.

9. Be aware that kids (and adults) learn and train in different ways and at different speeds and mistakes are an important part of learning.

Not everyone learns at the same pace and past experiences will influence all aspects of their learning. Individuals who have participated in other sports or in activities like dance, often have better body awareness and they might catch on quicker. Some will like having a routine or steps to follow; others will insist on doing it their own way.

Process is more important than outcome. I teach that part of archery is learning to shoot every shot the same way and the easiest way to do that is with a series of steps. For some archers we use the NTS (National Training System), for others we use a much simpler routine (e.g. stance, draw, anchor, aim, release). What is chosen depends on the archer, and what the archer wants to accomplish. We tell archers and parents that good outcomes come from good process, and without good process, good outcomes won't happen. (This is very difficult for some archers and some parents to understand and so is constantly reinforced.)

Athletes need to learn a skill before practicing it. You can't send them out to practice aiming if you haven't taught them how to aim or made sure they already know how to do it. Make sure they know the fundamentals before moving on. Look for the athlete's strengths and build on them. It's more effective to build new habits than to try to break old ones. Keep your feedback short and simple. Use cues and triggers, but make sure the athletes know what they mean.

Remember that we learn when we make mistakes and help your archers (and your parents) to remember it as well. Kids (and adults) know when they've made a mistake, there is no need to point it out to the rest of the world. When appropriate, let the kids figure out how to fix the mistake themselves; support them and help them figure it out if they can't.

Some archers will train better alone; others train better in groups. Some may prefer a couple of days a week; some may prefer longer sessions less often.

Training and practice sessions can sometimes be hard and not a lot of fun. Try to end the session on a fun note. Depending on the group you are coaching, it might be an archery game or it could be head-to-head matches.

10. Teach (learn) during practice; perform during competition. Many athletes go into a competition thinking they are going to shoot a personal best or they're going to try something new. It's best to discourage these ideas and help the athlete realize that shooting their average and shooting their normal shot during a competition are good things. Try new things long enough before a competition so that they are natural when the competition comes around. They use what they learn at practice to perform at the competition.

During the competition, the coach can support the archer, and maybe give short cues to help the archer remember specific things, but hovering and commenting and evaluating every shot is generally not very helpful. Make some notes and maybe some video, and discuss it at the next practice Encourage parents to let the archer decide when to talk about all that happened and try to make that time not at the competition and not on the ride home!

11. Create new leaders and instructors and share what you know. Older and more experienced archers can be great instructors and role models for your less experienced archers. This can happen both formally and informally. Formally, you can have team captains; informally, you can ask archers to help each other or help you.

We've had many of our older students get certified as instructors and had them help us teach the younger students. It's been a great first job for many of them and while they are learning to teach, they also learn a lot that can help their own archery.

As you go to more advanced coaching classes and seminars, share what you've learned with other coaches and your students. You can also become an instructor/coach trainer and teach other coaches and you'll learn a lot yourself while you're doing it!

Chapter 18 Some Deeper Thoughts on Coaching

These are some ideas and concepts that have come from many of the coaches I've worked with, books I've read, and things I learned in schools. I won't thank all of the people involved, because there are just too many of them and I might forget someone!

☙ ❧

Teach your archers how to do it right. Telling archers what they are doing wrong isn't always necessary, especially the beginners. I want them to focus on doing it right, so that's what we talk about. Sometimes more advanced archers don't understand what I'm trying to change, so then I will explain what I am seeing, but I always finish by explaining how to do it the right way.

Catch them doing it right. This can be behavior or it can be form. We tend to only comment to kids when they are doing something wrong so I try to find things they are doing right. That might be helping someone else, changing the cardboard or the targets, or being quiet on the shooting line.

☙ ❧

Avoid using these four words – *don't, but, just, try*. All of these words can cause more problems than they solve. When we say: "Don't think about pink elephants" we think about pink elephants. It's much more effective to say: "Think about blue and purple elephants." It's the same with archery: "Keep your bow arm pointing at the target." is much more effective than "Don't drop your bow arm."

When we use "but," it negates whatever was said before. If we say "That was a really good release, but. . . ," we all forget the first part and instead hear what comes after "but." Use "and" instead or even better, stop after the compliment. "That was a really good release. Do it again and keep your shoulder down," could be good; but "That was a really good release. Do it again," is even better.

"Just" just isn't necessary. Most sentences and comments are a lot better without using "just." Try it and see!

"Try" is a hard thing to do. Like Yoda said: "Do or do not, there is no 'try.'" For example, "try" to sit in a chair. You either do it or you don't; so what does it mean to try? It is the same with everything else.

☙ ❧

Use systems, not goals. For a lot of people, setting goals doesn't work. Others tend to sabotage themselves. Some are lost once they have met their goal or they give up if they don't. I prefer a discussion about "how." It's very similar to goal setting, but not as much of the SMART stuff (SMART goals are Specific, Measurable, Attainable, Realistic, and Time-based). The end result (or goal) might be to get to the next achievement level or win at a competition, but for either one, the system could be shooting 100 good arrows every day, focusing on a specific part of the form. If I follow the system I will improve. Record keeping is still necessary, and scoring regularly for measurement to see if the "system" is working is important. Of course, for those who prefer to have SMART goals, using a system will help them as well.

Coaching happens at practice; performance happens at the competition. Most of my work is during practice or training, making sure the athletes are ready for competition. I explain this to the athletes and their parents ahead of time so that they know I will be there if they need something during a competition, but I'm not going to hover, and I'm not going to make changes. I also explain that there will be other coaches at the competition and sometimes they will comment to the athletes or make suggestions. I will tell the athletes to listen politely, and let the other person know that they have a plan and they will share their suggestion with me. We can then discuss it at the next practice.

Shoot your average at a competition. If athletes try to shoot the highest score they've ever shot at a competition, they will probably be changing something. I encourage them to follow their process every shot and shoot their average. If they do shoot a personal best it's an extra reward!

If instructions are necessary at a competition, keep them short and simple; use cue words and signals. This is self explanatory; however, it is important that the athlete knows what those cue words and signals mean. Use the same words and signals during training so the athletes understand.

Focus on good shots. Often, if an archer shoots five tens and an eight, all they think about and talk about is the eight. I encourage them to focus on the five good shots and how they happened. Some will get so caught up with the one bad shot, that it's almost impossible to get them out of the downward spiral. Experience and reality checks are the best teachers.

ര ഇ

Remember that getting "good" takes work. Getting good is not easy and sometimes it's not fun. I often have to remind athletes that they have done hard stuff before and they can do it again. I also remind them that making changes will mean their groups get bigger, but they will come back together. I'll talk with them about frustration and mistakes and that they are both okay and part of learning. The word "yet" comes in handy here, for example "you haven't shot your 250 . . . yet"

ര ഇ

I am a resource . . . the archer has to do the work. I can't make the archer do the work. I can make sure they have everything they need. I can help put together training plans, but it is up to them to do the work . . . and let me know what else they need.

ര ഇ

Use the focus, distraction control, and meditation techniques you teach your athletes. Coaches need to be calm and focused. There are lots of things that happen at competitions and you need to be calm enough to deal with them. If you blow up because a judge made a mistake, it won't do any one any good. If you can take a deep breath or count to ten, or use another technique you've practiced, you can reason calmly with that judge and possibly work things out.

ര ഇ

Take a time out if you need it. Sometimes things happen and you need to get away. Better to get away than to say or do something you might regret. Sometimes getting your focus and calmness back requires an escape. Let another coach or parent know what you're doing and escape for a few minutes.

USA
Rio2016
Atos

Chapter 19
My Coaching Bag

Traveling internationally as a coach over the last few years, there were lots of things I learned to take with me, and have the athletes take with them. Sometimes they seemed kind of silly or unnecessary, but they often came in handy. I didn't take all of it with me if we were in the USA, because the trips were usually shorter and there was usually a shopping center nearby. At least one coach on each trip had a complete tool bag and most archers also had their own tools. Below I have listed the non-equipment related items that I took with me. I started out using a backpack; I switched to a small roller bag because it was easier to find things, it held more, and it was much easier to carry.

Stuff I Took On The Field,
But the Athletes Didn't Necessarily Need

American Flags I usually carried at least two. They were large flags – about 3 feet by 5 feet. They marked our area under the tents; and, at one tournament, the organizers had not been able to find one so they used one of ours. (I didn't need these at USA events!)

Portable Power Supplies for Phones and/or Tablets A lot of tournaments now put out information electronically, and if you need to keep your phone on all day it might run out of power. I made sure I had enough extra power to last at least eight hours. I also took a small thumb drive and an adapter so I could use it with my phone. I only used it a couple of times, but it was nice to have when I did need it.

Small Notebook I kept all sorts of notes, from target assignments to things I wanted to bring up at a team meeting. It was a lot easier (and more efficient) than trying to remember everything.

Easy to Eat Snacks Athletes would take their own snacks but some days went a lot longer than expected and they would run out. I had extra nutrition bars (ProBars or Cliff Bars or something similar) in case anyone needed them. I avoided anything that would melt (e.g. chocolate), or that would make their hands sticky (e.g. oranges).

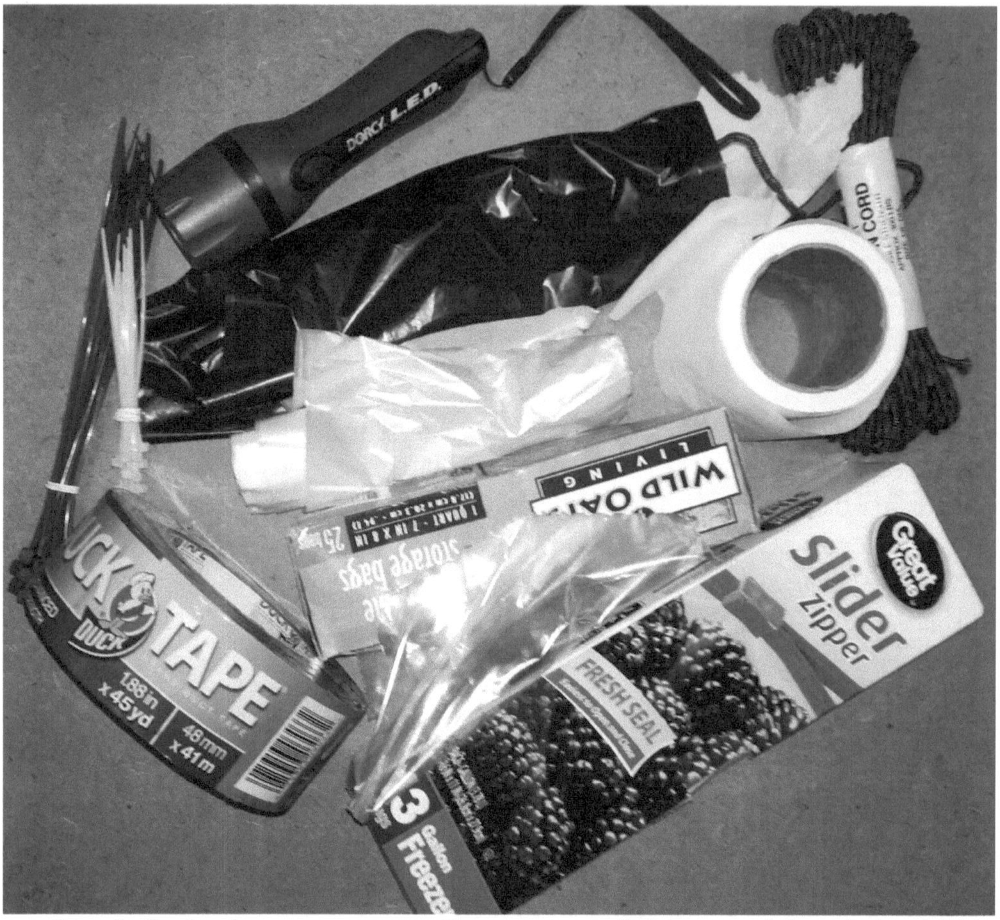

Small Cooler Ice was very often not available outside of the USA, but even if it was not available, a small cooler could keep things out of the sun and a little bit cooler. When ice was available, we put some in plastic bags to stay clean for drinks, or to be ready for icing sore muscles. The snacks were packed in the cooler for travel.

Peanut Butter When I started traveling with the Para Team I would take two large jars of peanut butter, but international food improved, so I stopped taking that much. It was usually easy to find bread and jam or honey, so we could make sandwiches if we needed them. It's also good with apples or bananas. (If you take peanut butter, make sure you pack it so TSA can get to it easily. I also recommend you put it inside a plastic bag.)

Safety Pins and Alligator Clips They can be used to attach competitor numbers (either to a shirt or quiver) and they can also be used to keep clothing out of the way.

Markers in a Couple of Colors We used them to put names on water bottles (in a lot of places, the water bottles were liter-sized, and each team member got one or two for the day). This way not as much was wasted. They could also be used to mark equipment (we marked with names and USA) or make signs. I always included at least one silver marker in case we needed to mark arrows.

Copies of passports, travel itineraries, classification cards, correspondence and copies of receipts from the organizing committee These have come in handy many times and I was glad I had them. I stopped taking the paper copies but I had copies on my phone and my iPad. I made sure they were actually on my device and would be available even if we didn't have Wi-Fi; the internet was not always available.

Stuff I Took For The Hotel, But the Athletes Didn't Necessarily Need

Doorstop Very handy in hotels, especially if I needed to meet with athletes and didn't want the door closed. It also signified "open" hours, if athletes wanted to come chat.

Thank You Notes and Thank You Gifts A gift for the organizing committee was usually provided by USA Archery, but often there were others I wanted to thank: a great bus driver, an interpreter, or someone at the hotel. I usually had the team sign a couple of targets that could be used as gifts as well.

Adapters, Converters, and Charging Cords and Plugs I took spares of these; someone would usually forget theirs or need a spare.

My Own Towel and Pillowcase I took my own towel because I never knew what there would be in the hotel. I didn't always like the smell of the laundry soap used in hotels, so the pillowcase helped with that as well. For both, I made sure they were an unusual color, something that most likely wouldn't be mistaken as belonging to the hotel.

Office Supplies I learned about taking these from one of our first team managers (Thanks, Kim!). I took a plastic storage container with tape, scissors, stapler, post-it notes, extra pens and pencils, paper clips, rubber bands, etc. It stayed with my travel stuff so I could just grab it and I didn't have to re-create it for every trip. (I would often take this back and forth from the field to the hotel.)

Stuff I Recommended For Everyone

Duct Tape Duct tape is one of those "not so valuable" items that can be "very valuable" when you need it! It can be used to cover trademarks, repair bow cases and quivers, and even hold up the flag. We even used it a couple of times to hold damaged suitcases together.

Flashlight Another item that might not get used often, but when you need it, it's nice to have a flashlight.

Toilet Paper or Tissues Just in case there isn't any where you're going! (Body wipes can be nice as well.) This was often kept in the bow case – the hotels usually had it, but sometimes the portable toilets on the field would run out.

Disinfecting Wipes These have become much more important and should go in carry ons as well as in bow cases. They can be used to clean off airplane trays and windows (if you're going to lean against them), water taps, and door handles.

Plastic Bags in Lots of Sizes Garbage bags can be used as rain gear in an emergency or they can keep a wheelchair cushion dry. They can also be used to cover backpacks and bow cases from the weather. Smaller ones can be used for snacks (to take something from breakfast for a mid-morning snack), or to cover scopes while not shooting, or to take wet stuff home.

Snacks Days can be long and the meals provided by the organizers are sometimes not what's needed or wanted. Snacks they are familiar with that can help keep sugar levels where they need to be are what we recommend. Food that is sticky, messy, or melts is not recommended unless it stays in the hotel.

For the Weather

A Sun Hat It can be just as important to have a hat to keep the sun out of the eyes and keep the head a little cooler. If necessary, ice can be put in the hat to do some rapid cooling.

A Warm Hat If it's cold, a warm hat can make a big difference. Athletes usually bring hats to keep the sun out of their eyes, but sometimes warmth is just as important.

Gloves and Hand Warmers Again, both are nice when it's cold!

Inclement Weather Gear I bring one set to keep me warm and one set to keep me dry. If necessary, I can use both. I encourage athletes to bring both as well and to bring stuff they know they can shoot in. Some will prefer to get wet especially if it's warm, but they will want dry stuff when they are done shooting.

Microfiber/absorbent Towels These come in handy if the weather is bad. They can be used to dry equipment and people.

Books or Games or Music with Headphones At most Para events there is a lot of waiting, especially for buses, and sometimes the bus rides are long. Having something to do that doesn't bother others is a good idea. They are also nice between rounds or during breaks.

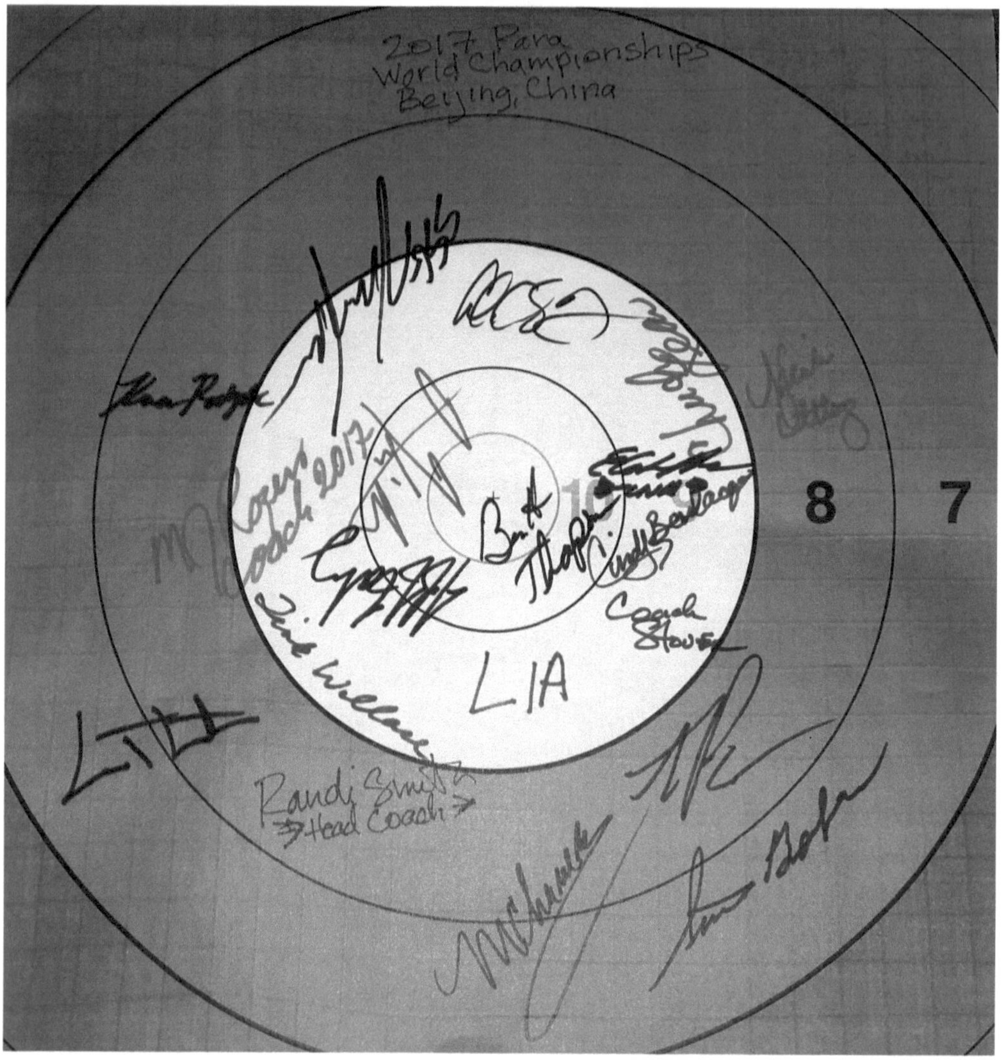

Note—I had a packing list I would give to coaches and athletes when trips were to be taken. I provide those lists at the end of this book in Resources.

Chapter 20
Mental Training for Coaches

Why Do Coaches Need Mental Training?

Coaching can be exciting, and occasionally boring, but along with exciting and boring, it's also often stressful. Many of the things we train athletes for, we need to train ourselves for as well. The "stage" for the coach's "performance" is different, but the needs are the same. As with the athletes, skills need to be practiced and used in many different situations.

I found that constructive self-talk and being aware of, and then controlling, my breathing and body tension were the most important tools for me. If I realized my neck or shoulders were tensing up or I was starting to feel stressed or overwhelmed, I was usually able to take a few deep breaths and talk to myself to calm down.

Probably the most important reason that coaches need to know mental training techniques and need to be able to practice them is so that the athletes know the coaches have the skills to help them (the athletes) if they are having issues. Along the same line, coaches need to know how to remain calm and confident so they can help their athletes stay on track or get back on track if necessary. Athletes will have a lot more confidence in their coach if they are able to practice what they preach.

There are many books and videos available to help you learn these skills, therefore I am not going to cover how to learn them. Following are some examples of times you might need mental training skills. For most of these examples, self-talk and controlled breathing are the most important skills to learn and use. At the end of this chapter I'll provide a list of some of my favorite resources.

Coaches Need These Skills

To Stay Calm Under Pressure Maybe an official makes a call you don't agree with and it makes a difference in the outcome. Can you calm down enough to have a civil conversation with the official and not get kicked off the field? There can also be pressure when there are several matches going on at the same time and you need to keep track of everyone.

To Deal with Distractions/To Focus On What You Need to Be Focused On Have you ever been helping an athlete with something and you hear a noise or see a crowd and you lose track of what you're doing? Maybe something is happening at the other end of the field, but you need to stay focused on your end. One time you really need this skill is when you are in the coach's box during a big match. You need to watch the clock and the athlete you are coaching, not the other athlete.

To Be Able to Adapt If you want your athletes to be able to adapt to schedule changes, nasty food, rain delays, and all the other stuff that can happen, you need to be able to do it as well. Getting angry and stomping off because the target assignments need to be adjusted, or because the clock broke, isn't good for your athletes or for you. Being able to calm down so you can look at the situation objectively, and then deal with it will make a big difference for both you and your team.

To Hide Your Feelings An athlete, or a parent, or another coach might say something that makes you angry or hurt, but it might not be the time or place to deal with it. At this point, you'll need to stay calm and file it away so if necessary, you can deal with it later. Again, if you are in the coach's box, you need to be able to hide your reactions from others, both positive and negative. Sometimes you might need to put on that calm, cool, and collected face, and go take a timeout!

Staying in the Present Thinking about the match going on right now can be a challenge when you know there is another match or some other event coming up later - or if one is going on at the same time. If you have an athlete who needs medical attention or has an equipment issue, it can be hard to delegate that to someone else. Being able to keep your focus where it needs to be is important. Remember and use the acronym WIN – What's Important Now.

What Skills Will be Most Helpful?

Breathing For me, learning breathing techniques to control my activation level was really valuable. I'm generally fairly calm on the outside, but being able to be calm on the inside, as well, was very valuable. Focusing on breathing (long breaths in, longer breaths out) can take your mind off of other things and allow you to reset. With practice, it can work fairly quickly.

Self-Talk Being able to talk to yourself - whether to calm yourself down or psych yourself up - is a valuable coaching skill. Talk to yourself like you're talking to a friend - give yourself the same advice, in the same manner that you would give someone else. For example, be stern if you need to and specific, but don't be a bully!

Routines & Checklists This can be as simple as making sure you have everything in your backpack, or it can be as complex as you want to make it. For me, I liked to go through and find target assignments and time schedules for all of the athletes the night before. Depending on the event, I might make the list just for myself, other times I would make a copy of the list for all of the coaches. I could figure out which coaches would be with be which athletes - and knowing all of that was done, would make sleep a little bit easier.

What to Teach Athletes

As a coach, you can teach the athletes to use some mental skills as they learn to shoot. What you teach will depend on the level of the athlete and your own skills. All of these skills can be fairly basic or they can be more detailed when appropriate.

1. ***Help athletes with their self talk.*** It's surprising how many archers come into their first lessons thinking this is going to be

easy, and when it's not, they get down on themselves. They may start saying they're no good at this or it's too hard. You can help with reinforcing the ideas that getting good takes time and work. You can use the concept of "yet," by reminding them that even the best archers were beginners at one point and help them turn around what they are saying. Have them put a list of positive statements in their quiver so they can pull it out when they need it.

2. ***Help athletes learn to be aware of stress and how to deal with it.*** Help them learn what the body does and maybe help them realize that they can look at it as excitement, not nervousness. You can explain that if they are nervous, it's because they care and it's important to them.
3. ***Assist them in putting together routines.*** You can start with a routine for each shot and a routine for putting their equipment together. As they advance you can add routines for reset, pre-shot, and pre-comp - many archers don't see the importance of any of these, but as they get more advanced, if you continue to talk about why they use them (helps make sure they remember everything, confidence is knowing they're ready, able to get back to where they need to be) they may be more willing. Have them write down their shot routine and put it in their quiver so they can pull it out when they need to.
4. ***Learn about the how and why of journaling or keeping notes.*** Equipment changes, knowing what they have and what changes they make. I suggest using the last page of their journal or notebook for important notes (like sight markings) that they might need more often.
5. ***You can help them practice relaxation, imagery, and visualization skills.*** You can find relaxation scripts on the web or you can make up your own. I found that once they had learned to relax, using kids' books to help them visualize was one way to help them understand what visualizing is. Box breathing (breathe in for a count of four. hold their breath for a count of four, exhale for four, hold their breath for four, and then repeat) is easy to teach. You can increase the count to help with relaxation or resetting.
6. ***You can provide situations where they can practice the skills you've been teaching them.*** Make noises to distract them, play music they don't like, talk about them while they are shooting. Let them know that they need to practice staying focused on their shot process, rather than what you are doing.
7. ***They can learn how to use WIN (What's Important Now) and forget what else is going on.*** This might be with group dis-

cussions, or it might be an individual conversation when you see that an archer is distracted. It can sometimes help if you explain that the brain doesn't think about more than one thing at a time very effectively, and they can choose what to think about.

Resources

- ***Headstrong Consulting*** (headstrongconsulting.com) They also have a podcast called "Becoming Headstrong"
- ***USOPC Coaching Education*** https://www.teamusa.org/About-the-USOPC/Coaching-Education
- **Don't Leave the Mind Behind** by Keith Henschen and Nicole Detling (book)
- **In Pursuit of Excellence** by Terry Orlick (book)

Chapter 21
Self-Talk—What You Say and How You Say It Matters

When you consider that you spend more time with "your self" than you do with any other person in your life, it's a good idea to keep track of what you are saying to "your self." Most people talk to themselves all day long and athletes are no exception. This internal dialogue is called self-talk and can serve many purposes. Self-talk is used by many successful athletes to help monitor, instruct, and encourage themselves.

Self-talk is an important part of managing a mental performance system. It can help athletes stay focused on the present, deal with stress, build confidence, and improve self-image. Self-talk can correct bad habits, prepare for performance, focus attention, create a positive, constructive mood, and build confidence and competence. It can be used to instruct or encourage, as part of a pre-competition or competition routine, and to increase or decrease activation. Self-talk can help the athlete's actions become automatic, allowing them to feel and sense their way to a peak performance.

Self-talk can help us forgive ourselves and get back on track when we make mistakes. Often it is not the mistakes themselves that hold us back; it is our reactions to the mistakes. Learning to deal with failing and making mistakes is an important part of being a successful athlete. Having a "reset" or "mistake recovery program" is important. Some people will physically "brush it off" by brushing their shoulders or "throw it away" by imaging putting it in their hand and then actually throwing it. Other ideas have included using visualization and "flushing it," "parking it," or "filing it" until later.

Whatever it is, a self-talk strategy needs to be something that works for the archer, breaks negative patterns, and doesn't interfere with performances. It also needs to be practiced so that it will work when it's needed.

Research has shown that the words we use when we talk to our-

selves are also very important. When changing a behavior, using "I don't" instead of "I can't" can make a big difference. For example, instead of saying "I can't eat junk food" use "I don't eat junk food." It's a simple thing, but it takes the negotiating out of the statement and makes it easier to follow. It changes something from being imposed upon you from without, to a decision you have made from within. Other examples might be "I don't miss practice," and "I don't skip breakfast." You can also make an "I can't" or "I don't" statement into a positive statement, such as "I eat healthy foods" or " I remember to write in my journal."

Research has also shown that talking to yourself as a friend, using the second person, can be effective. This could manifest itself as saying "you can do this" instead of "I can do this." This turns you into a supportive friend and leads to less anxiety and more confidence. We all tend to talk to our friends nicer than we talk to ourselves! It can also be more powerful because it reminds us of advice from others and makes our self-advice more objective and helpful.

Here are some ideas to keep your self-talk more constructive and helpful. Be sure to practice these so they are effective when you need to use them.

Listen to yourself; what do you say to yourself about yourself? We talk to ourselves constantly. We have more input into our own lives than anyone else. Is what you are saying helping or hurting?

How we frame our self-talk can make a big difference. When we say we're nervous and/or scared, our body reacts: our palms sweat, our heart beats faster, adrenalin clouds our thinking, and we function less well, putting our bodies under great stress. We can "reframe" and look at it as being "excited." The body reacts the same, but we interpret it differently.

Think about a growth mindset and not being able to do things "yet." We might have a fixed mindset when we believe we can't do something, or we can have a growth mindset and believe we can learn. With a fixed mindset, we might give up and tell ourselves "I can't do this, so I'm going to quit trying." With a growth mindset, we understand that the brain is like a muscle and is continually growing and changing and we will get better with practice, so we can be more encouraging and say "I don't know how to do this yet, but I can figure it out."

Figure out what works for you. You can probably figure out cues that you can use during practice and performances that will work and help you remember what you need to do. For a reset, "erase it" or "park it" might work. While shooting, something like "stay strong" or "stay smooth" could work. Try to use the same cues during practice that you will use during a competition.

Tell yourself what to do instead of what not to do. Instead of telling yourself "don't drop your bow arm" tell yourself to keep "both sides strong." Focusing on what went wrong is basically creating instructions to repeat what went wrong. Always focus on "doing it right."

Try changing "I can't" to "I don't." This can be a really easy way to change some habits or behaviors, especially when combined with telling yourself what to do. Tell yourself "I don't eat sugary foods; I eat healthy foods instead."

Make sure you are seeing the whole picture. Self-talk can be so powerful, it overwhelms other input, including reality. You might be so busy thinking about how badly you are shooting that you don't realize you're on the way to a personal best. Or you might be so focused on that one bad arrow, that you don't see the five good ones!

Learn to pay attention to what you are saying and learn to reset. Negative self-talk gets loudest when you need it the least. Learn to recognize what you are saying to yourself about yourself and come up with a way to make it better. Sometimes a list of positive statements that you have prepared ahead of time and can pull out of your quiver will help.

Talk to yourself like you would talk to someone else. The things we say to ourselves may be things we would never say to our best friend - so why do we say them? Self-talk is more effective when you do it in second person, using "you" instead of "I." For example, say to yourself "you can take three deep breaths and relax." Using your name can be even more effective.

Remember that very few things happen "always" or "never." We tend to think in superlatives – always or never – and very few things always happen or never happen. For example, "I'll never get all of the arrows in the yellow" or "I always lose in elimination rounds." Use all the skills listed above and say something else!

Most Importantly—We Can Change and Improve the Way We Talk To Our "Self." Listen To Yourself—When Necessary, Correct Yourself and Make It Better!

Joe's Story

by Joe Bailey

I was in a very severe semi-truck accident that left me with massive blood loss, a full leg amputation, compression back fractures and a head injury. I spent two months in a Rehab Hospital and then three more months learning to walk on an artificial limb.

Just 11 months after completing truck driving school, I found myself needing a new career. I went back to school three years later for a degree in Engineering Design and tried again to get work.

After the accident, but while still in rehab and using a wheelchair, I made it into my old bedroom and got my 80 pound hunting bow out. I quickly figured out I could still pull it!

A few months later I started my personal archery rehab and found an outdoor archery course where I could practice outdoors because my main interest was still hunting. We practiced outdoors using broadheads on cardboard animal targets. After that summer and after hunting season, I started indoor archery shooting, primarily NFAA leagues (animals and 5-spots) and 3-spot Vegas targets. That turned into a 33 year addiction!

That next summer I started 3-D shooting on the IBO Circuit. Shoots were held all around Michigan. I was able to attend outdoor

shoots and work on getting my confidence back so I could trust my ability to take game with my archery gear!

For a couple of years I volunteered to run a target league. I now had three addictions: indoor, IBO, and outdoor, no matter what the weather! I found I liked big bull's-eye targets at long distances with long stabilizers. That all led up to me shooting at Outdoor Nationals one year, when it was in Michigan. It was a double FITA; 4 days of shooting. We shot 90 and 70 meters on the first day, 50 and 30 meters on the second day, and repeated that on the third and fourth days. After the four days of shooting, the top 64 males and the top 64 females shot elimination rounds until they had a winner. It was basically a week long marathon of shooting in summer weather conditions!

After a week of shooting, I missed first place by one point! The good thing was, I met other disabled archers and people that I shot with for the next 14 years!

In 2001 I started my disabled archery career after being invited to a U.S. Olympic Training Center by the U.S. Paralympic Coach. He had watched me shoot and saw that my scores were high enough.

At my first international shoot, my string loop broke just minutes before my individual match, so I was out of shooting until the team round. As a team, we were very successful and we won the Gold Medal in the Open Compound category and set a new world record. After having self-funded to the World Championships and being unable to shoot in the 2004 Athens Olympic Games, I was ready to retire from the US Disabled Team. (Note Open Compound was not in the Athens Games.)

In 2005, the International Paralympic Committee added my shooting style (Open Compound) to the Beijing Paralympic Games for 2008, so I thought about it and decided I could do three more years and try to make the Beijing team! I made the team and ended up 6th in qualifications and 5th overall. (I was taken out in the quarterfinals by my teammate, T.J. Pemberton!) I ended up that year as the #1 ranked archer in the USA; and #6 internationally.

Two weeks after the Games, all of the USA Paralympic and Olympic athletes were invited to the White House. The whole thing was an unbelievable experience I will never forget!

I have many trophies and medals from all over the world and the USA and they all live in a bag with the memories of hard work and crazy travels. However, the things that I really won are teammates and coaches who were all playing for the same goal and who have gone on to become lifelong friends, who I am still in touch with today!

Chapter 22
Coaching at National Tournaments

A lot of coaches believe coaching at a tournament is the same as coaching at practice, however, I think they are actually quite different. Coaching at the various levels also has differences, and I'll try to discuss them all: individual, club team, and national/international teams.

The first thing I need to do is come up with some definitions for the words I will be using. So. . . .

Performing is what the athletes do during a competition. It is using all the skills they have learned during practice.

Coaching is what happens at a competition to help the archer perform and use what they have learned at practice. It also happens at other times, but at the tournament it is more of a support, helping the archer remember and use what they have already learned.

Practice is the time to learn new things and try new things; time for the coach to teach form, tournament skills, and get the archer ready to perform.

Teaching is what happens at practice. It's a very important part of a coach's job, but usually only happens at practice. This is when the archer learns to use mental skills as well as shooting skills. It is also when they learn about tournaments and how they work.

Being a coach comes with many different roles: teacher, listener, motivator, problem-solver. Most of them can happen both at practice and competitions, but I believe that teaching happens mostly during practice. Coaching can happen at both practice and competitions. I explain to athletes that their job during a competition is to perform and to use what they have learned; my job is to be there if they need something and to help them remember what they have learned. Coaching does not include being with the athlete 100% of the time, and as an archer advances they need may still need coaching but the type of coaching changes.

Part of my own philosophy has always been that athletes need to be responsible for their own performance. My job is to help them learn the skills to get to that point. This means that I also need to explain my philosophy to athletes and parents (or significant others) so they don't think I'm not paying attention or ignoring them. I also let the support crew (parents, partners, friends, etc.) know what they can do to help support the athletes; for example, maybe one part of their form they can watch for and help the athlete remember.

To help the athlete be responsible for their own performance, I try to:

1. Make sure they can be comfortable on their own. I do this by starting them out at local tournaments and running club tournaments like bigger tournaments.
2. Teach them the skills needed to be on their own: how to set up and take down their bow, how to adjust their own bow sight, how to mentally reset after a bad shot, how to deal with distractions. We do all of this at practices and the local tournaments. As they advance, the skills get more advanced as well.
3. Make sure they know how a tournament works. They need to know how to score, how to call a judge, and what to do if they have an equipment failure. They also need to know the basics like whistle signals, and line etiquette. We double score at practices and talk about all the other things that might happen.
4. Explain that at a competition other coaches may suggest a change or a new technique to them. These other coaches are usually trying to be helpful, but it's not the right time to be taking suggestions. I suggest that they listen politely, and then tell the other coach they will talk it over with me. I explain that changing something during a competition (unless it's an emergency) is not a good idea.
5. Let them know that sometimes when they get stressed or get frustrated, lots of people (including me) may give them more information than they want or need. In that case, it is okay for the athletes to tell me it's too much info or they can tell me to "go to my office."

Of course, all of this doesn't happen at the first tournament, and I'm going to be interacting with them a lot more when they start to shoot than when they've had lots of experience.

Before the tournament, we discuss what's important for them at the tournament. It may be just to experience a tournament; it may be maintaining their form during the tournament. It is very seldom the outcome (score or place) that is important. It may take several explanations and several tournaments before the archers (and their parents) really understand what it means to not focus on score, and how difficult it is, but it is important to keep doing it and it's important that words and actions after the tournament reinforce this concept. (We explain and remind the archers and their parents that for things to go correctly at the target, things have to be done correctly at the shooting line.)

Related to focusing on process, we also talk about the idea of "shooting their average" at a tournament. A tournament is not the place to have a goal of shooting a new personal best; instead, it is a place for the archer to do what they have been doing. A new personal best is a nice bonus, but they need to be aiming to shoot their average. We also discuss that a goal of medaling is also not a good goal because they can't control that. They could shoot the best score they've ever shot and someone else could shoot a higher one. (At a certain point, placement might be a goal, but hopefully by that time, they understand the concept of focusing on process!)

We talk about what will happen at the tournament and what they should have with them. I explain that at some tournaments there is a designated seating area for athletes, and athletes may or may not (depending on the tournament) need to stay in that area. Archers can usually walk back and visit with parents and spectators, but it's often easier for the archer to have their snacks and drinks with them in the athlete area.

At the Tournament (With JOAD Kids or Individual Athletes)

For tournaments in the USA, the individual athletes make their own travel arrangements. I often recommend a specific hotel, but the athletes can stay somewhere else. We generally eat some meals together, but not all of them. We use texting to make sure everyone knows the schedule and what is going on.

At the competition, I make sure I know which targets the athletes are on, and I make sure they know where I will be. I may be socializing, or walking up and down the field, but I keep track of them. This gets difficult at some tournaments when there is more than one field, that's when texting can come in handy. If they have parents or others with them, I also give them my contact information, just in case they need something.

As I walk up and down the field, I make sure athletes have food and water, and I get them some if they need it. If they want me to stay and watch, I do that as well. I might remind them about a specific

part of their shot, using cues we've worked out at practice and that are short and to the point. Those cues are always specific, such as "keep your arm pointing at the target." Vague statements such as "shoot your shot" aren't very helpful, and I've found they can cause stress that isn't needed.

I don't ask about score or placement, but I might ask if their arrows are grouping. This is usually after I've been watching for a bit and I know what their arrows are doing. If I notice a definite pattern (for example, everything to the right), I might mention that what I have seen is all their arrows going right and it might be a good idea to adjust their sight. (Only when I know the archer well and it's an important event, will I actually tell an archer to move their sight.)

One big thing I see at tournaments is over-coaching, by both parents and coaches. (*Note* When I refer to parents, I'm including spouses, partners, and anyone else who may be there supporting the archer.) Some things I think both coaches and parents need to remember include:

- Let the coach be the coach and the parent be the parent. Kids need both; it's important that each one do their job. It's hard for one person to do both.
- When coaching, use specific cues. Make sure the archers know what the cues mean (figure this out at practice). If you tell them to remember to transfer and they have no clue what transfer means, it's going to hinder more than it helps. Remember also, the cues need to tell them what to do, not what not to do (for example, tell them to "set your head" instead of "don't move your head").
- I sometimes see archers go back to the waiting line after every end

to talk with coaches or parents. When this is for socializing, it's seldom a problem. However, occasionally I see the coach or parent trying to analyze every shot: why this one went right, why that one was high, and of course, reminding archers that they need to focus or concentrate harder. (Have you ever tried to concentrate harder? It's not very easy. Learning to focus and refocus comes with practice. There's a lot going on at tournaments. It's not the time to learn!)

- What if an archer has a breakdown? Breakdowns are usually caused by expectations, maybe the parents', but usually the archer's. For example, they may expect to shoot their USAT (US Archery Team) score, but have several bad ends, making it unlikely to happen. I can support them, and I usually start by asking them to shoot—paying attention to their process—so I can see if I can spot an issue. If I can, we can fix it and move on. Often though, I find the problem is due to over-thinking or over-analyzing. The archer has a bad end and starts trying to figure out why, and because they are trying so hard to figure it out, they aren't able to focus on their process. The more they try to fix it, the worse it gets. This is a downward spiral. If they are trying to analyze after every shot, I'll suggest they start looking for patterns after every three arrows or every six arrows. I've also been known to have them put scopes in the waiting area so they can't use them after every shot.
- The way to solve both of these issues is to get their thinking back onto their process. However, this is much easier said than done. I give archers a specific part of their form to think about and encourage them to forget about the score. It'd like to be able to say it always works, but it only works sometimes. There are times when the best I can do is to let the archer know I'm there and I'm watching, and assure them that we will figure it out at the next practice. Again, telling them to focus harder or concentrate harder doesn't work; it often makes things worse.
- Parents and coaches: make sure you know why your archer is participating in archery. Is it to be with friends, have fun, and learn a skill? (Those are the three reasons most people participate.) If the archer's goals are different from what their support crew thinks they are, it can cause unintended conflicts.
- Coaches: make sure the support crew knows what you are telling the archers and they know what the tournament goal is. I've worked with archers for whom the goal was to get through the tournament without a temper tantrum. This can be a lot harder

than it sounds, and if the parents don't know that is the goal, they can inadvertently cause a tantrum.

- Parents - for many kids who participate in sports (not just archery), the kids will state the time they hate the most is the ride home. On the drive home, let the kids guide the discussion. They know if they did or didn't do well, but they may not want to talk about it for a while. Maybe food or ice cream is a better idea! You can always ask if they made friends, or if they had fun, or if anything interesting happened.
- At all tournaments, things can get stressful and days can be long. As coaches, we need to remember to take care of ourselves. We need to make sure we are drinking (water), eating, and getting enough sleep. We need to have the skills to control our own emotions, to be able to listen – sometimes to many people at once – and to admit when we don't know the answer. Coaches need mental training as much as the athletes do, but we forget.

At the Tournament (With a Team)

A lot of what I do as a team coach is similar to being an individual coach, but there are some major differences. Things don't always work as I want them to, but this is what I aim for!

When our teams travel within the USA, it's not much different from working as an individual coach. Many of the athletes have coaches with them, so I check in with them and do a lot of watching so that I do know the archer's form. At the end of the tournament, I may make some suggestions as to what to work on until I see them the next time. If an archer is having an issue or has questions, I'll always try to help, but sometimes the answer is "Let's talk about it after the tournament."

When traveling with teams, the times between shooting (meal times for example) can be as important as the shooting. These are good times to work on team bonding by spending time together. It might be by doing some sight-seeing or it might be by going to a restaurant together. We've gone to movies, gone deep-sea fishing, and done lots of shopping!

Chapter 23
Coaching at International Tournaments

International events for the para-archers definitely had some different issues. I liked having the athletes fly as a group from the USA, so we would meet at a USA airport and fly out. This made it possible for coaches to help athletes get on to the plane and help with getting all of the athletes' stuff into the plane. Athletes would take their own wheelchairs to the plane entrance and then they would be gate checked and returned when we landed. This also made it possible for the coaches to help with folding and re-assembling the chairs so that all of the parts got back where they belonged.

Transportation to and from the airport and the field was always one of the more stressful parts of the trip. Most countries had only one bus with lifts or ramps and there were a lot of athletes who needed them. Scheduling could be tight, but the officials always made sure everyone had made it to the field before shooting started.

One of the biggest was often accessibility. Most countries don't have the laws that we have regarding access, so we'd often end up having to share the shower in one accessible room - on one trip, the athletes using wheelchairs actually showered in a locker room.

Packing for the trip was different as well. Several of the athletes took their own shower chairs and they had to be sure to have enough medical supplies for the duration of the trip. Keeping luggage at the weight limit could be a definite challenge. We also had to be prepared for all types of weather and we carried plenty of snacks with us as well. I had a packing list for me and one for the athletes that I sent out before each trip. (See Resources the end of book for a copy of these.)

Getting Ready to Get There

Just as with individual athletes, I wanted the team to be responsible for their own individual performances. We worked to prepare the athletes and coaches for this as well. Some of the things we worked on (mostly during training camps) included:

1. *Learning to Trust Themselves*
   Athletes need to know they may not always have a coach standing behind them and if they do have one, that coach may not be the coach they are used to. Because of that, athletes need to be able to spot their own arrows and know how to deal with distractions and how to reset after a bad shot.
2. *Learning to Communicate*
   Athletes need to be able to tell coaches what information they want, when they want it, and when they need more or less information. They need to learn how to be specific about what they do or don't need. Along with this, coaches need to be able to accept it when the athletes don't want/need the information they are providing or when they are giving too much info at one time. This isn't always easy for the coaches, but when they understand that the goal is for the athlete to be successful and our job is to help that happen, it can help.
3. *Getting to Know One Another*
   When coaches know the athletes and the athletes know the coaches, things go more smoothly. Some coaches may be personal coaches for at least a couple of the athletes, so they know those athletes well. However, all the coaches need to work at getting to know all the athletes and their shooting form so they can help the athlete if necessary. If there is a new team coach traveling with the team, the other coaches can help them out with this. Spending time as a team doing non-shooting activities, from dinner as a team, to occasional sight seeing can help with everyone getting to know each other better.
4. *Learning to Work as a Team During Team Rounds*
   Archery is generally considered an individual sport. Archers spend a lot of time training on their own so learning to work as a team can take some work. There is also a possibility that the team at the event may not be the same people who have been practicing as a team at home. When together, having different groups shoot together and shooting in different orders helps to find the best groups and the best shooting order. Some athletes do better in the first position; some are better able to handle the stress of time running out and can shoot last. Simulating equipment failures, timing failures, and yellow cards, can help the team be more prepared if those things do happen.
5. *Learning to be a Team*

The para teams I worked with were pretty solid teams and they supported each other and generally enjoyed being with each other. At training camps, we did non-archery activities to get to know one another. At tournaments, because of the logistics, we usually traveled together and ate together. It's a lot easier when everyone can get along. Looking out for each other and cheering each other on were important.

6. *Being Prepared*
   During training, simulating all the things that can go wrong at a competition before the competition helps confidence levels by helping athletes know what to do if there is a problem. We do mock tournaments, and have the athletes switch to back up bows mid-tournament. We have target assignment mess-ups, clock malfunctions, noise, equipment malfunctions (simulated), and anything else we can think of. We discuss all the things that can go wrong and how to be prepared.

At the Event

When a team travels out of the USA, the staffing is different from what it is at most training camps. There are more coaches; there may be a team manager; and there can also be other staff such as sport psychologists and athletic trainers. The staff need to work as a team

as well, so it's important that they be able to communicate with each other.

One job of the Head Coach is to look at each day's schedule and make assignments for the other coaches and staff. They need to know who is going to do what (and where and when). I tried not to give the team manager, the sport psychologist, or the medical staff any other responsibilities, so they could be available if necessary. They would all help with pulling arrows during practice, but they needed to be available when the athletes needed them. (Some teams have the team manager make these assignments; I preferred to do it myself.)

Some athletes had personal coaches with them. I had our team manager sit down with the personal coaches and explain what they could and couldn't do. We were often able to get field credentials for the personal coaches, so they could help with scoring and pulling arrows, but if the tournament organizers were limiting who was allowed on the field, personal coaches were the ones most likely to have to watch from the sidelines. We made sure to explain to the personal coaches that they were acting as the archers' agents, so they needed to call judges when necessary and pay attention to the scoring.

Training and Official Practice

Practice time was usually scheduled at international tournaments. Open practice was sometimes available before the official start of the competition so I would try to arrive two to three days before official practice so we could adjust to the time change and the food. We adjusted our schedule to the time zone we were in as soon as we arrived—no naps, staying up until normal bedtime, and getting up early the next morning. We would go practice and often stay at the field as late as we could in order to avoid sleeping. Within a day, the team had usually adjusted to the shift in time zone.

Depending on the transportation availability and scheduling, members of the team shooting in the afternoon could choose to come on a later bus or they could take the early bus. Transportation was always one of the big unknowns—would all of the busses be wheelchair accessible or would there be two sets of busses? Would there be a set schedule or could we request the times we wanted? At least one staff person would go to the field on the earliest bus to secure a spot for the team and start bringing out equipment.

Official practice usually ran on the same schedule as the qualification schedule. Equipment inspection took place during official practice. The officials would call the team over all together. We gathered

up bows (primary and backup) and assistive devices and headed over as a group. All the athletes had to have their classification cards with them as well. Fortunately, they now accept an electronic version, so the athletes can have a copy of their card on their phone. The "card" is actually a sheet of paper, so they have that in their bow case, in case they do need it.

Athletes using stools or wheelchairs have to fit them and their equipment into a designated space, so there was usually an area taped out for the athletes to show that they fit. Compound shooters also had to pull back their bows to make sure they met the weight requirement. Several members of the team were unable to hold the scale and their bow, so coaches would pull back the bows for them. Uniforms were also checked during equipment inspection. Visually impaired archers who were using masks also had their masks checked.

Qualification Rounds

The qualification rounds (sometimes called ranking rounds) at international tournaments are run like the qualification rounds at our USA events. There is usually more than one session; there might be three or four. For me, it was important to be at every session (and I liked to be there!). I usually assigned coaches to specific athletes and sometimes they all didn't need to be at every session, but I was fortunate enough to work with a great group of coaches and they usually stuck around for every session even if their presence was not necessary. Athletes could pull and score their own arrows if they chose to, but coaches would score and pull the arrows for most of the athletes. If athletes had problems during the qualification round, we watched and tried to use the same cues that we had used during training. It was important not to change anything or give them anything new to think about. Generally, the biggest issue was over-thinking or over-analyzing, so getting the athlete back to focusing on process was usually the goal.

The qualification round determined placement and positions for the elimination rounds.

Elimination Rounds

Before the elimination rounds, I talked with each of the athletes to find out if they had a preference as to which coach would be behind them during the matches. I explained that they might not get that coach, but I wanted to know if they had a preference. I did the same thing with teams and asked them to communicate with each other and come up with a first and second choice. It was not important to me that I be behind the archers, sometimes they were more comfortable with other coaches.

After I had that information, either the team manager or I would make notecards for each of the coaches showing when and where each athlete would be. Athletes often started at different times so we all had to know when and where everyone would be. Fortunately, at most tournaments, once the brackets were published, we could find which target the athlete started at, and by following the bracket, we could tell where they would go if they won the match. The athletes' name plates that were at the targets also had the information on them.

The information that I previously listed under "Learning to Communicate" became even more important during elimination rounds. Coaches communicated ahead of time with athletes to find out what information they needed. Some athletes wanted nothing other than a countdown from 10 seconds or five seconds. Others wanted reminders, maybe to keep their bow arm strong. Again, it's important that coaches paid attention to these requests; doing something different could distract the archer.

Finals

International events often have a different format during the finals (medal) matches. They may be at a different venue, and the archers usually don't go score their own arrows. This added a couple of new issues to deal with.

There is often an announcer whose job it is to keep the audience informed. When the announcer tells the audience that Archer A needs a ten to win, or that if Archer B shoots an 8 it could go to a shoot off, the archer needs to be able to ignore it. We worked with the archers during training to help them learn to ignore the announcers and during the competitions we would keep the archers occupied with small talk during the scoring. (We had a couple of archers on the team who were pretty good at being announcers so we could practice during training camps.)

If the finals are at a different venue, there is a small practice area nearby and practice time is scheduled and limited. With experience, the archers learn to deal with this, but it was something we needed to make sure the new archers were aware of and they were prepared. They would be summoned to the finals field one or two matches before theirs, which meant standing around and waiting. Some athletes listened to music and some liked to watch the previous match, but it was also a good time to make a trip to the restroom. We had worked out ahead of time which coach would be with which archer, so they could work together during the practice time. This was a time to review the cues (if necessary) and confirm when the archer wanted the timing countdown to begin.

During the finals there is an agent down range scoring the arrows. This means the archers could be standing around doing nothing between ends, but the time between ends was short. I would come up with a way to intentionally keep the archers' minds off the score, whether it was doing math (count from 6 by 7s) or telling stories. It was also a good time to make sure they were drinking water.

When an agent was down range doing the scoring, the archer would get their arrows returned every other end, so they needed to have enough to shoot two ends (2 x 3 = 6; plus at least one extra). The agent knew they were acting on behalf of the archer so they could call for a judge just as the archer would do. If an arrow was damaged (e.g. the nock was broken), the agent sent the arrow back upside down, so the coach and archer knew there was a problem. The agent needed to make sure that once he handed the arrows to the runner, the runner didn't turn the arrow right side up!

After the tournament was over, we tried to have a team dinner or team dessert and a wrap up session. We also used this time to let everyone know what the arrangements were to get to the airport and when they needed to be ready to go.

Other Happenings

Over my years as a Head Coach, I developed ways I liked to do things. These were things that were important to me. Some of these could be considered Team Manager responsibilities, and I would often do them with the Team Manager. When I first took over the Para Archery Team, we often traveled without a manager, so I did both jobs and found what worked for me.

- If even just one of the athletes on the team was competing, I wanted to be on the field. There might have been another coach with the athlete, but I would still be there. The only exception was if I was working with an archer who had an upcoming match and I was on the practice field.
- If one of the athletes had to be classified or got selected for anti-doping, I had someone go with the athlete. It was usually the athletic trainer, but if they weren't available, either I or one of the other staff would go with them. Both classification and anti-doping can be stressful; I thought the support was important.
- I ate with the athletes or after the athletes. For lunch, I would often grab something at breakfast and then stay on the field during lunch. I could watch equipment and sometimes it was a chance to rest and reset.
- I had snacks for me, but I also kept easy to eat snacks in my bag in

case an athlete (or another coach) needed one. We had long days when the archers went through all of their own snacks and mine were needed. Protein bars, little bags of almonds or other nuts, and jerky were easy to carry.

- I usually took the last bus back to the hotel. That way I could be there if there was some sort of problem and I could make sure that everyone else made it back.
- I was very much aware that my attitude could be easily transmitted to the team. If I was angry or frustrated, I did my best to keep it hidden. Most of the time, I was pretty successful. When necessary, I'd let another coach know I was taking a time-out and I'd go for a walk.

Chapter 24
Help With Tournament Organization / Accessibility Issues for Tournaments

Tournament season is always coming up and as more and more archers who use adaptive equipment are shooting, more and more tournament organizers (who are often coaches) are wanting to make their tournaments more accessible for adaptive and para-archers.

Definitions

Para-archers are archers who have been through the classification process and have an official Para-archery classification. Adaptive archers may be Paralympic-eligible but they have not been classified. They may also not be eligible to be classified or they went through classification and were found to be Not Eligible. However, they may still use a chair or other adaptive aids.

USA Archery has a policy making it easier for archers using chairs and stools to shoot in competitions. Those with classifications are able to shoot in Para categories; those without classifications can still use stools, chairs, or wheelchairs, but they don't shoot in Para categories.

Some Helpful Ideas

Here are some ideas divided into three segments: how to make an official tournament (like a state or national tournament) more friendly, how to make a local or club tournament more accessible, and how to put together a competition for archers with disabilities.

Official Tournaments

My definition of an official tournament is a tournament that needs to stick to certain rules, so there is not a lot of room for flexibility in the format or the categories. This would include national championships, team selection tournaments, and tournaments that are used for ranking purposes.

How can you make an official tournament more friendly?

Start with making sure archers using wheelchairs, walkers, crutches, etc., can get where they need to go. How far is it from parking to registration? From the registration area to where they will be shooting? Parking to the shooting line? Shooting line to restrooms? Where are the concession stands? How far are they from parking and the shooting line? Where and how are scorecards turned in? Where is equipment inspection?

Along with looking at where everything is and how far apart it all is, look at the terrain and the surfaces. Gravel paths are great for normal walking, but they are nasty for people using wheelchairs or crutches. Long grass and wet grass are also difficult to push a wheelchair over. Are there steps? If so, is there another way of access that is still a reasonable distance without steps? What looks like a small hill to someone walking, can be a major obstacle to someone in a wheelchair.

What about restrooms? Are they accessible? Do they meet ADA standards? Are they close enough? If they are portable restrooms, the same questions apply. The access into a portable restroom is also important; make sure it is accessible.

Sharing information such as target assignments, current scores, and schedules can be an issue. Having this information online helps a lot, but not all tournaments are able to provide online information. Most schedules and target assignments are posted at four to five feet off the ground, in tiny print. Both of these are understandable, but it would be much nicer if they were low enough and big enough print for people in wheelchairs, short people, and people with visual impairments.

Target assignments are an important issue as well; para- and adaptive archers should not be separated from other archers, they should be mixed in on the lines. Most archers who use wheelchairs and stools prefer to stay on the line (especially outdoors) instead of coming on and off the line after each end. When putting target assignments together, if tournament organizers put three people on each target that has someone who stays on the line (instead of four), the archer who stays on the line can be on either the right or left side, and the other two archers alternate on the other side. Often the other archers on the target will help score and pull the arrows for the archer who stays back, which can reduce the need for agents. Be aware that archers with visual impairments will need to set up their equipment ahead of time and when possible should be able to keep their equipment set up throughout the competition.

Information provided on the registration form can help the organizers with target assignments. Include on the forms somewhere for athletes to let you know if they use stools or wheelchairs and if they stay on the line or come on and off. All archers who shoot in VI classes will have equipment that needs to stay on the line.

Awards and banquets are important as well and organizers need to think about them. Is the award stand accessible to archers using wheelchairs? If not, is there a different way to do the awards? Is the banquet area accessible? If awards are given at the banquet, is the presentation area accessible? What kind of tables are there? Picnic tables are hard to get under or slide onto. Is there space between tables for those who need extra room? Is it a buffet? Do you have someone who can help carry plates?

Local and Club Tournaments

Local and club tournament organizers need to think of everything mentioned above, but they probably have more flexibility. If they have an archer come in who doesn't fit in the regular categories, they can make another category. (Many states already do this with Peewee or Yeoman categories.) They can include shorter distances for archers who can't reach official distances.

Although accessibility is still important, the set up for the tourna-

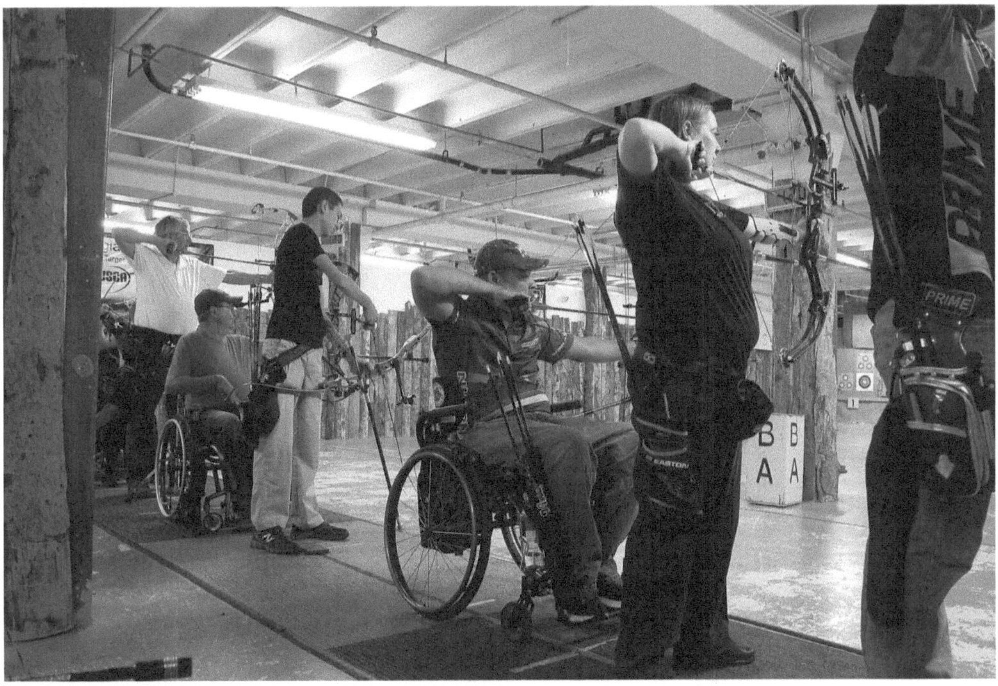

ment is usually not as complex, making adaptations much easier.

Competitions Only for Archers with Disabilities

There are many organizations (Move United Junior Nationals and the Warrior Games are two examples) now putting on events for athletes with disabilities and many of them include archery. These can be a different sort of challenge because of the range of disabilities and experience.

We have found it works well to include official distances, but add a novice distance. Everyone can shoot at the same time, but by having the novices shoot shorter distances, the time spent prospecting for missed arrows is reduced and the archers have a lot more fun.

A format we have used successfully with adults is to have the advanced/intermediate competitors at official distances (50 m for compound; 70 m for recurve) and the novices all at 30 meters with an 80 cm target for compounds and a 122 cm target for recurves. If kids are shooting, targets can be placed at appropriate distances for them.

Scoring and pulling arrows at a tournament specifically for archers with disabilities can be a challenge. Sometimes a group of volunteers can be recruited and trained to keep score. Categories for awards can also be adapted by the organizers.

Chapter 25
Running an
Adaptive Archery Clinic

As soon as you become known as a coach who works with disabled archers, you will get asked to do clinics for adaptive archers! But don't immediately shy away, running a "try me" clinic for archers who have disabilities is a lot of fun. It takes patience, creativity, preparation, and hopefully, some volunteers! It also takes a willingness to think "outside the box" and an ability to adapt on the fly.

Once you've been asked and/or decided to do a clinic, you'll need some initial information. This article will guide you through the information you'll need and how you can run the clinic. These ideas have worked for me - and I've done lots and lots of these clinics!

Initial Information You Will Need

- *Where will it be held?* It may be a gym or a park; your sponsor may have a general idea, but want some input from you.
- *How many participants are expected?* As you get more information, make sure this is a realistic number that fits with all of the other requirements: space, equipment, time, etc.
- *Ages & Disabilities* You may not get specifics at this time, but you can get a general idea. You can find out if it will be young kids, older kids, adults, or a mixed group.
- *Format* Will it be one group for an extended time; more groups for a shorter time; or will archers be shooting just a couple of ends and then moving on? Will there be other activities going on? Other activities may not make a difference, but participants may be coming and going and you are going to want to make sure none of the other activities are set up in such a way as to make your activity unsafe.
- *Do they have equipment available?* What kind, what size, how much? Is the equipment appropriate for the group? You'll need to be aware of draw weights and archer sizes. I always take a couple

of very light (both physical weight and draw weight) recurve bows. Genesis compound bows are great for groups, but they are physically heavy.

- *Who is providing the equipment?* Target matts, faces, bows, arrows, etc. If they are providing it, make sure you get specifics so you can be sure it is appropriate. If you are going to provide it, make sure what you have is appropriate.
- *Volunteers* Are they available, will they need training? (See note on volunteers.)
- *Accessibility* Hopefully they have already thought about this, but you'll need to make sure the archers can get to the shooting area and restrooms, weather protection, and water are available.
- *Awards* Will there be scoring and/or awards? Do you need to worry about them or will the event organizers handle it?

After you have all of this information, you can decide if you are able to do the event. If not, maybe you can recommend someone who can do it, or you can find someone to help you so you can do it.

Note on Volunteers At many events where clinics are offered, the volunteers might have no experience with archery. The organization hosting the event will most likely take care of getting the volunteers, but you will need to train them. It is actually fairly easy to train the volunteers to help the archers shoot, but you need to make sure the organizers have them arrive early enough to get trained. They need to know basic safety rules and very basic archery. If they get there early enough for them to shoot a couple of ends, it will help a lot. Don't expect the volunteers to be certified instructors or coaches!

Planning The Event (and sometimes before you actually commit to do the event)

- If possible, visit the site. Find out where the targets will be, where the shooting line will be and the shooters will be. Check for safety in all directions and let the organizers know if they will need to make any changes.
- If they are providing the equipment, try to see it before the event. Even photos will do. Clarify who will be setting up the equipment and make sure they know what you want and need. Verify that they actually have enough and it is in safe shooting condition.
- If you are providing the equipment, do an inventory and figure out

if you will need to add anything or do any repairs.

- Try to enlist a couple of your own volunteers/assistants. How many you need will depend on the ages, disabilities, and number of participants. Volunteers who you know you can trust and who know what they are doing, will make things easier for you. It works out well if you can train one of your volunteers to train the other volunteers on the day of the event.
- Double check all of the initial information and make sure nothing has changed. Find out if they have specific requests. Some examples may include wanting to keep some sort of score. Keeping a list or tally of how many archers is fairly common.
- If they want awards, make sure you know who is providing them and determine how many you will need.

Planning is Vital, But . . . I also find that very often these events don't run as planned. The first year we did clinics at the Endeavor Games, many of the kids were scheduled for their swimming events during the time they were also scheduled for archery. The pool happened to be in the same building, so the kids would shoot a couple of ends, do their swim event, and come back and finish. Other years we had archers arrive late because of another event. Make sure your registration coordinator and traffic coordinator can handle stress and can adapt if necessary!

What You Will Need

- At least one table
- Chairs—for spectators, archers who are waiting, but also for archers who need to sit to shoot
- Markers for the shooting line and waiting line. Outdoors, paint is the best: indoors, tape works well, but make sure it is safe for the floor. Often, if you are in a gym, you can find lines already on the floor that will work.
- Target matts and stands
- Bows, arrows, armguards, finger tabs or gloves, releases (I use trigger releases with wrist straps). If I'm using light bows and the archers are not going to be shooting a lot of arrows, I may not start with finger tabs - but I always insist on armguards and I prefer the long ones that go past the elbow. Finger tabs can be more distracting than useful. I do always have them available for anyone who does want them.

- Something to use as quivers (commercial ground quivers, 18″ plastic cones, etc.)
- Something to use for a bow stand or a place to put the bows when they are not being shot.
- Target faces and target pins. It's more fun to be able to hit the target, so we use large targets at close distances.
- Safety flags or tape to mark off safety areas
- Pencils, pens, score cards, clipboards
- Depending on the location, you may need some sort of archery curtain and/or some sort of shade (canopy, etc.)
- Awards
- Adapting stuff
- Releases – trigger releases with wrist straps are the best
- Strapping – PT gait straps, webbing, elastic bandages – all of them will work
- Quad gloves – from Active Hands – you can use elastic bandages, but the quad gloves are much easier
- Have a tripod with a sight attached and something to use as a foot marker for archers with visual impairments. Even easier, have a bow stand/sight stand made by Archery Shooter Systems . This stand can also be used to hold a bow for archers who cannot hold their own.
- 550 cord for mouth tabs (make simple mouth tabs ahead of time—*see Chapter 8 for construction instructions*).

At The Event

Finally, the big day arrives!

Before The Participants Arrive

- Set up the shooting line, target line, and safety line. If you are shooting outside, start with your targets close enough so that archers are not likely to miss. This will keep arrows from getting broken and reduce the time needed to search for arrows. Twenty yards Is a good distance for adults; ten yards for kids.
- Mark off the shooting area and safety areas with safety flags or tape. Appoint a range captain whose ONLY job is to watch the range and blow the whistle. If you have a large group, you may need two. Make sure they are communicating with each other.
- Train and/or orient the volunteers. After you've explained to everyone the process you'll be using, assign specific jobs to specific volunteers. For example, assign someone to the registration desk, someone as range captain, and someone as shooting line coordi-

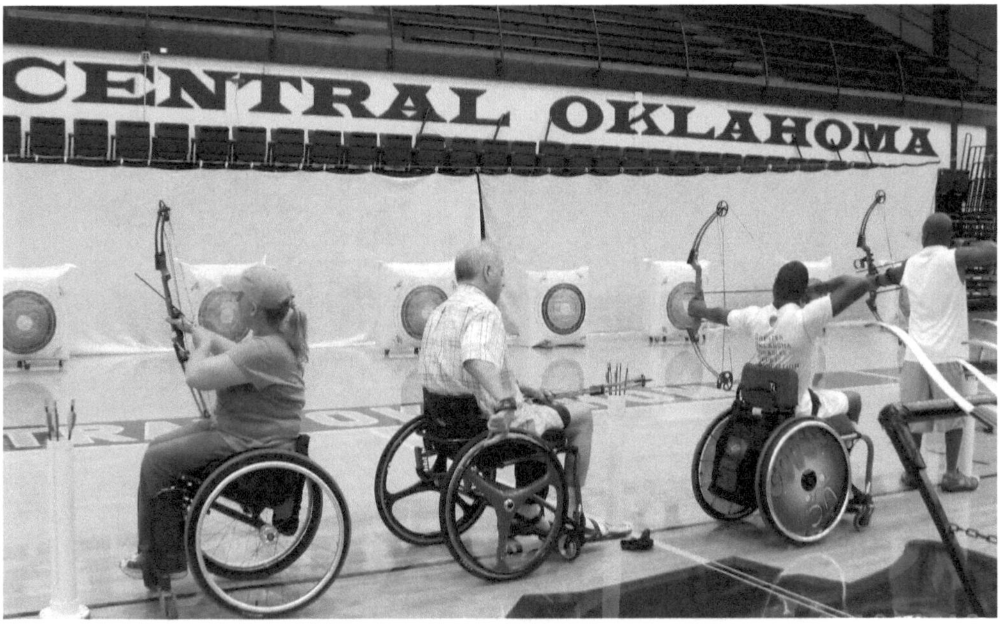

nator. You can the do the training for the specific jobs.

- You will also need instructors and arrow pullers. For some archers, the instructor and the puller will be the same person and they will work with one archer as long as the archer is shooting. Other archers may need instruction for only one or two ends and then only someone to pull arrows. There may also be some who can be completely independent once they receive the basic instruction.
- The volunteers who are doing the instructing and pulling need to know the safety rules, the basics of teaching, and they need to know how to pull and carry arrows. (See note on volunteers)
- If the organizers want the archers to keep score, this is a good time to teach the volunteers how to score.
- With the volunteers who will be doing registration and depending on the format, figure out a check in system. They can get necessary record keeping info (names, zip codes, etc) and assign a volunteer to help each archer. You might need a designated area for archers who are waiting to shoot.
- Having a volunteer expediter can be very helpful. This person can jump in when things get bogged down to get things flowing again. (They need to get out of the way as soon as they have helped get things back on track so the instructors don't feel their job was butted in on.)

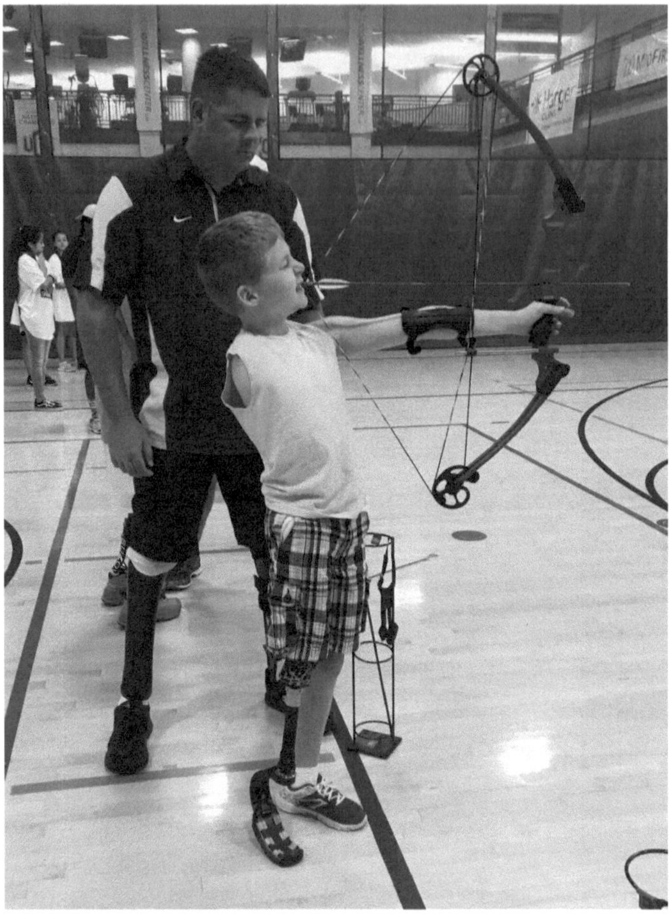

As The Participants Arrive

(In this section, I am referring to the volunteers by the jobs they are performing)

- Have the participants check in with the registration desk. The volunteer at the registration desk can assign a volunteer to help them and show them where to wait until an instructor is available.
- The instructor can explain the process and the safety rules to the archer. Depending on the experience of the instructor, either they, or someone you have specifically assigned, can get the equipment for the archer and determine what (if any) adaptive equipment is necessary.
- The shooting line coordinator can assign a shooting spot (or lane) to the archer and the instructor can help the archer get set up and ready to shoot.
- Once everyone is ready to shoot and the range is clear, the range captain can give the signal to shoot. Archers will shoot their arrows with whatever assistance they need. When they are finished shooting, the bows can go on the rack, or if appropriate, the archer

can hold the bow in their lap.

- When all archers have finished shooting, the range captain can give the signal and the arrows can be scored and/or retrieved.
- The process can be repeated before a new set of archers is ready to shoot.

When the archers don't all arrive and finish at the same time, the shooting line coordinator's job is to keep track of which lanes are open so that newcomers can be assigned. In this case, the coordinator can help with equipment, but it can be difficult for them to do any other job. If the group starts and stops all together, the coordinator can sometimes have other responsibilities as well.

Awards

At clinics, awards are not always necessary; the participation is enough. If you are giving out awards, determine ahead of time what awards will be given and how they will be given out. There are several different ways they can be done; here are some ideas.

If you are not keeping scores:

- Provide souvenirs to all participants. It's usually best not to consider these as awards. Sometimes sponsors provide giveaways that can be given to participants. You can also include information on where to find more information and who to contact if they want to follow up.
- Awards for certain performances, maybe an award for hitting the yellow or having all their arrows in the red or better.
- Photos If you have an instant camera or someone who can print photos as they are taken, photos at a target (designated for photos) can be fun.

If you are keeping scores:

- You'll need to decide on categories for awards. It might be just high scores. It could be categories based on age, gender, and/or disability. You might include the type of bow (if more than one type is available). If you are using an award stand or podium, make sure that all archers can get to it and on it. If that's not possible, don't use it!
- Usually when I do clinics, if we're using awards, I'll have a general idea of how I want to do them so I can get a count of how many I will need. Then at the event I'll have the person doing registration include name, gender, age, bow type, and any sort of assistive equipment (wheelchair, chair, mouth tab, release) on the scorecard. We can then decide on the awards based on who is shooting. I will sometimes also add a novice division if I have both new

shooters and more experienced shooters.

After You're Done

Remember to thank your volunteers! As you're cleaning up it can be helpful to either put aside or make notes about any equipment that needs to be repaired or replaced. Get it repaired as soon as possible and it will be ready for next time. If you have time, you can check with the volunteers and maybe the participants and see what they would change for next time.

Resources

- ***Active Hands*** activehands.com. (also available on Amazon.com)
- ***Archery Shooter Systems*** bowhanger.com (if you want the VI stand, you'll have to specify that in your order)

Chapter 26
Purchasing Equipment

So, you have adaptive archers who have decided they want to buy a bow. They tried archery and thought it was a lot of fun!

The best approach is to have them go to a local archery shop and get some help, but sometimes the employees at the shop won't have all of the knowledge they need to get the archer the right equipment. Because of the archer's disability they might not shoot in the traditional manner; the manner the employees are used to dealing with. You might find it best to go with the archer to the shop, or help the archer determine exactly what they need.

If you don't have a nearby shop and they need to order online, make sure you help them determine the correct equipment. It may be difficult to return anything that is not correct.

Recurve or Compound Bow?

The type of bow the archer is looking for (recurve bows and compound bows are the most common) most likely will have been decided by the time they are ready to buy a bow. If not, with your help, they can look at what they are going to be doing with the bow and what their interests are. Some things to keep in mind are:

- If it's a recurve bow they want, make sure they start with a low enough draw weight, typically at a draw weight less than what they think they need. If the riser they choose allows for some adjustability, it's possible to go a little heavier, then adjust the limbs to the lowest weight. We often recommend buying a three-piece recurve bow with a good riser/handle and less expensive limbs. Once their form is good (and maybe they've stopped growing!) and you know what the best draw weight is for them, then have them buy higher quality limbs. Make sure you know what kind of limbs the handle needs; some bows will only take one brand of limbs; others take many. If the archer, plans on using a recurve bow for hunting, be aware of minimum draw weights, but everyone works up to those levels and they will need to also. Do not start the archer at that draw weight; it will inhibit learning to shoot well!

- If it's a compound bow they want, get one that has a great deal of adjustment both in draw length and draw weight. Some bows can adjust draw length without changing the weight, but others will increase in weight as the draw length increases - make sure you get the one you want. As they shoot more, they will probably stretch out and probably get stronger. As they perfect their form, their draw length may change as well. It's also good to consider the amount of let-off; some target shooters prefer a lower let-off.
- Another alternative is a universal or zero let-off bow (Genesis being a brand name of a popular bow of this type). Genesis bows are used in the National Archery in the Schools (NASP) program and they are a good beginner bow. It's also a great bow if they are going going to share it, perhaps with others in their family.
- A cross-bow is a fourth alternative. They may be legal for hunting in some areas for people who have disabilities. They can be difficult to cock and load, so that is also something to keep in mind.

Factors Affecting the Fit

How the archer holds the bow and holds the string is critical to the fit. For archers who have disabilities, which hand does what is not always determined by which hand or eye is dominant (such as being "right-handed" or "left-eyed"). They may have to select whether to get a right-handed or left-handed bow based on which hand holds the bow better, or which one pulls the string better. (The terms right-handed and left-handed when applied to bows are determined by the hand/arm which pulls the string.)

How they will release the string is also critical to the fit. This is another part that needs to be considered as you consider bows. Here are the most common methods for archers who have disabilities:

- *Finger tabs or gloves with fingers directly on the bowstring* Finger tabs and gloves are used by most archers who shoot recurve bows and Genesis bows. There are several styles; it is important to make sure the finger tab fits and is comfortable when used.
- *Release Aids* Release aids typically provide a mechanical trigger to release the string and they are usually used by archers who are shooting compound bows, whether they are target shooting or bowhunting. A trigger release is usually used to start with. They are generally easy to use and come in models that can be strapped to the wrist as well as held in the hand. For those who can't use their fingers to set off the release, the trigger can be pushed against the chin or the cheek or another part of the face.

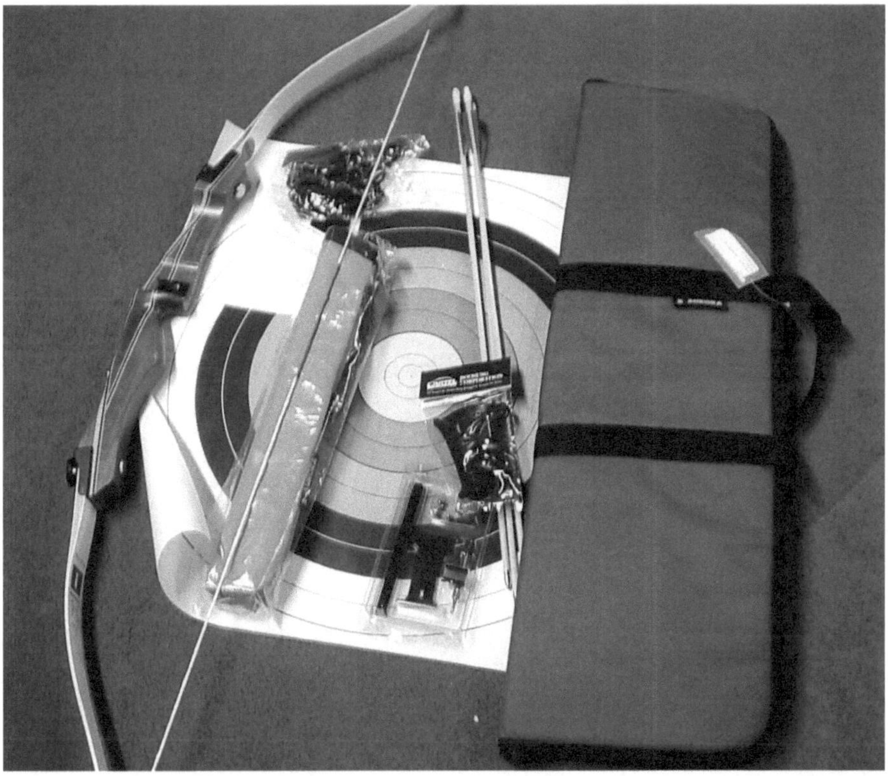

More advanced target archers often use thumb triggered or triggerless release aids, sometimes called "hinge releases." When trying these out, be sure to start up close. It can be a good idea to start with a strap or a release training aid. Things to consider include how it fits in the hand, how it hooks to the string, how it has to be held as the string is pulled back, and finally how the string is actually released.

- *Mouth Tabs* Mouth tabs are often one of the first methods tried by archers who have the use of only one arm. They are simple to make and use, but there are some precautions. It is important to make sure the archer starts with a very light-weight bow (draw weight) and the mouth tab is held by the molars, not the front teeth (*see Chapters 7-9 for more details*).
- *Shoulder Harnesses* Many archers who start with mouth tabs move into shoulder harnesses with releases attached to them. There are a lot of ways to release the string with a shoulder harness. They are custom made for each archer. They are becoming much more common and you can get some ideas by checking out Paralympic YouTube videos (*more specific information is in Chapter 10*).

Shooting from a Chair or Stool

If their balance is poor or they don't have a lot of endurance, consider shooting from a chair or stool. It doesn't need to be fancy, but it should be comfortable and ideally, it should allow the archer's feet to touch the floor/ground. Stools generally do not affect what kind of bow they get.

Shooting from a Wheelchair

If the archer intends to shoot from a wheelchair, the wheelchair itself is a very important part of their archery equipment. It should fit them and they should feel comfortable and stable. Here are other things to keep in mind:

- *Recurve Bows* Because these bows can be tall, make sure the string clears the bowside chair wheel at full draw. If the string presses on the arm of the chair, the push rim, or any other part of the chair it will affect the shot. If this kind of problem shows up, a shorter bow than would usually be recommended may be able to solve it. An extra wheel without a push rim could also be used. For some archers, putting a strap around their chest so they don't need to lean back quite as far will make them more stable and this may also solve the clearance issue. Pay attention to the physical weight of the bow and make sure balance and stability can be maintained.
- *Compound Bows* Usually chair wheel clearance is not an issue, but both the physical weight of the bow and the bow's draw weight need to be considered. The archer needs to be comfortable and stable. Beginners need to start with a lighter physical weight and a draw weight that is low enough to be pulled back safely with both control and good form.

What About Arrows?

There are many arrow manufacturers with all sorts of nocks and points. Be sure to consider the archer's budget and their experience level. Use your experience to determine what size arrows they need. With younger archers, you may want to get them a couple of inches long, so the archer can grow and still have arrows that fit (although if they grow too much, the arrow size may change also). Other options to consider include the type of vane, and the type of nock.

Other Accessories

There are many accessories available for both recurve and compound bows. To determine what an archer needs, you will need to use your experience as a coach. Be sure not to add too much too fast, but determine what they need just as you would with any other archer.

One of the biggest issues I find with equipment for all archers (not just disabled archers) is that they want too much too fast. They see an archer using something, and decide they need it as well – and that is often not the case. I try to explain why they don't need it and when they might. For example, they don't need a clicker until they have a consistent anchor – or they don't need a magnifying lens until they understand how to aim. Help the archer learn to manage their own equipment and what the different parts and accessories are for – and have fun doing it!

Chapter 27
Recreational Therapy and Adapted PE Goals

Some coaches who pick up this book may be running archery programs in settings such as VA Hospitals or rehab centers where having specific goals is an important part of all recreation programs. In these settings, archery is most likely part of the recreational therapy program. Archery could also be part of an Adapted PE program in which specific goals are also necessary. These goals are just as relevant for regular programs so the information could also be valuable for an ordinary archery coach who is wanting to start an archery program and wants to list some of the benefits of an archery program.

Why Archery?

Archery can be a great therapy tool. It can be done in a relatively small space; it can be an individual or group activity; it can be indoors or outdoors; and after the initial expense is a very inexpensive activity.

It's also an activity that can be quiet and calming or it can be loud and exciting. It can be competitive or it can be non-competitive. With some creativity, it can be a cooperative activity as well.

It's an activity that can be continued after rehab or school and it's an activity that whole families can participate in. It often needs little adapting, and it's an activity in which people who have disabilities can participate in with people who don't. Archers can choose to be recreational archers or they can choose to compete, from local tournaments to possibly the Olympics or Paralympics.

Within different types of archery, the amount of physical activity can vary as well. Standard target archery can vary from the archer staying in one place to shoot and someone else doing the retrieving of arrows, or the archer can do both. With 3-D archery, there is generally some walking, often on an improved path. Field archery usually has lots of walking, often in rather rough terrain.

I've listed some ideas for archery goals for recreational therapists, adaptive P.E. teachers, and anyone else who can use them. I have not put them in goal form because the format varies from place to place and there can be a lot of variation within each goal.

Recreational therapy, also known as therapeutic recreation, uses leisure activities to improve skills, abilities, overall health, and emotional well-being. It can be found in school settings, but is more frequently in community centers, VA Hospitals, and rehab centers.

Adaptive Physical Education is an adapted, or modified, physical education program designed to meet the individual gross motor needs, or other disability-related challenges, of an identified student.

Examples of Goals

Social Goals

Interact with one person
Interact with more than one person
Interact appropriately with one/more persons
Can participate as part of a group/class
Can find & set up their own equipment
Ask for help when needed
Can follow rules
Community participation
Can stay focused
Community re-integration
Can independently participate in archery
Can participate in small competition

Physical Goals

Can walk/wheel to targets
Can pull back light poundage bow
Can lift bow arm with bow with/without assistance
Can pull arrows
Stretching/ROM
Improve balance
Can put the arrow on the string
Can put the release/fingers on the string
Can hold the bow with/without assistance
Improve functional independence
Improve strength and physical fitness
Increase mobility, endurance

Emotional Goals
Can handle frustration
Improve self-esteem
Interact appropriately
Improve emotional regulation
Self management/responsibility: being on time, responsible for own medication, etc

Cognitive Goals
focus, memory, concentration
participate in goal setting
follow directions
improve problem solving
Can name the scores of individual arrows
Can write down the scores (or input them into an electronic device)
Can add the scores

Some Goals Can Fit Into More Than One Category
Can follow the steps to shoot 1 arrow /3 arrows /10 ends of 3 arrows
Goal setting
Coordination, balance, stability, discipline
Leisure activity

I've seen many benefits of archery with the archers of I've worked with. Some of these include:

Independence Several archers who started out with us, have been very hesitant about traveling on their own. One archer, after a few trips with the team, traveled by herself to South America to visit friends and family.

Purpose Many of the veterans who joined our program were able to attach a new purpose to their life. They were able to continue to serve the USA as they competed in international events. Several also started coaching and mentoring other veterans.

Self Advocacy For athletes who had always accepted things not being accessible or available, they gained the skills to advocate for themselves and others. This included getting equipment they needed and finding benefits they were entitled to.

Self Control Archery is a great activity for learning self control and anger management. Anger definitely does not contribute to consistent shots. Learning to recognize triggers, to reset, and handle things calmly were skills that were valuable in archery, but also carried over into everyday life.

Reduced Medications A few archers decided that the medications they were on were not really helping them and were able to reduce them. Others were able to find more effective medications.

Fitness Wanting to do well in competitions and to keep up with others helped several to improve their fitness levels.

Leadership This was one of the areas where athletes who had been in the military really showed their skills. Somewhat related to purpose, they were able to put the skills they had learned in the military to use in other areas. Many were on our advisory councils, several became certified coaches, and they encouraged others to serve as well.

Chapter 28
Adaptive Archery Q & A

Over the years I have fielded a great many questions about adaptive archery. When you get involved, so will you! Here are my answers to some of the most common question sent my way.

Archery is a great activity. It can be used for recreation, for therapy, for competition, or for all of the above. It's fun, almost everyone can do it, and it can be done as a family or group activity, or it can be done as an individual. People of many different levels can participate together; it can be done inside or outside, with basic group equipment or fancy individual equipment.

Competition is available at many levels starting with club shoots and going all the way to international events like the Paralympic Games. Regional multi-disability, multi-event competitions, such as the Endeavor Games, Texas Regional Games, and Thunder in the Valley Games give athletes with disabilities a chance to try out competition with others who have disabilities. USA Archery and the National Field Archery Association (NFAA) both offer large and small tournaments in which athletes who have disabilities are welcome to shoot.

What is the Difference between the Paralympics and the Special Olympics?

Paralympics and Special Olympics both provide competition for athletes who have disabilities. However, the populations served, the activities offered, and generally their overall purposes are different.

Special Olympics provides year round training and competition in many different sports. The population served is children and adults with intellectual disabilities (ID). The Special Olympics (www.specialolympics.org) website states:

The mission of Special Olympics is to provide year-round sports training and athletic competition in a variety of Olympic-type sports for children and adults with intellectual disabilities, giving them continuing opportunities to develop physical fitness, demonstrate courage, experi-

ence joy and participate in a sharing of gifts, skills and friendship with their families, other Special Olympics athletes and the community.

Special Olympics emphasizes participation and promotes the ideals of acceptance and inclusion through sport. There are summer and winter sports and they go from local to international competition levels. Athletes train and compete, but there is more emphasis on participation. At SO competitions athletes are matched with athletes of the same gender, about the same age, and of about the same ability (referred to as "divisioning"). There are over 30 Olympic-style sports offered.

Paralympics are like the Olympics, more about elite competition. ("Para" is parallel, so the Paralympics are parallel (similar) to the Olympics.) There are six main disability categories: amputee, cerebral palsy, intellectual impairment, visually impaired, spinal injuries and Les Autres (French for "the others", a category that includes conditions that do not fall into the categories mentioned before). Not all categories are included in all sports. Athletes go through a qualification and classification system in order to compete at the Paralympic Games.

The website of the International Paralympic Committee (www.paralympic.org) states their mission to be: *To lead the Paralympic movement, oversee the delivery of the Paralympic Games and support members to enable Para Athletes to achieve sporting excellence.*

In para-archery, the categories included are amputees, cerebral palsy, visually impaired, spinal injuries, and some Les Autres. Athletes go through a classification process where they are classified according to their disability (see the chapter on classification). Except for the Paralympic Games, International Para-archery competition is governed by World Archery. Archers with visual impairments are included in the World Championships, but not the Paralympic Games.

How do I Make a Paralympic Archery Team?

The process for making a Paralympic archery team varies from country to country but is often very similar to the process for making their Olympic teams. The country must first earn "slots" for the event. This is usually done at the World Championships and Continental qualifiers the year before the Games. If all slots are not distributed at those events, another event is held. For the USA, slots for the 2024 Games can be earned at the World Championships in Pilsen, Czech Republic in July and at the Continental Qualifying Tournament, the Para-Pan Am Games in Chile. USA can earn a maximum of two slots in each category. If we don't earn slots at those two events, we will have a final chance before the Games, probably at the World Qualification Tournament in Dubai in 2024. The process for other countries to earn slots is the same, although the continental tournament will vary

After a country has earned slots, the National Governing Body of that country determines how their country will decide who gets the slots. In order to make the 2024 USA team, the para-athletes will compete at the 2024 Arizona Cup and Gator Cup. After the Gator Cup, the top eight athletes in each category will compete in a third event which will be held immediately after the Gator Cup.

The following information applies to events that are considered Paralympic "pipeline" events. They are usually run by USA Archery or USA Archery clubs. There are other archery organizations that have different rules. If you are not in the USA, check with your National Governing Body for archery and/or Paralympic sports.

How Do I Get Started?

The best way to get started is to find an archery program or archery coach in your area. They very often have equipment you can try out to find if you really like the sport. They can also help you find equipment that fits and is appropriate for your level and help you adapt it if you need to. Once both you and the coach decide you are ready, you can start shooting competitions. If you're not sure where to look, you can look for clubs in your area on both the Move United and USA Archery websites.

Can Anyone with a Disability Be an Archer? What Is The Difference Between Adaptive Archery and Para-Archery?

Anyone with a disability can be an archer, but not all athletes with disabilities will qualify as para-archers. Para-archers need to fit into one of the categories listed above and they have to go through a classification process. Some archers who have disabilities who don't classify are called adaptive archers. These archers may use adaptive equipment (chairs are the most common), but they shoot with the non-disabled archers.

There are some tournaments open to anyone with a disability, for example the Endeavor Games, and they very often will use different categories or will add additional categories to the official categories.

And of course, not everyone who is an archer competes! There are lots of recreational opportunities such as leagues and clubs and different types of archery such as 3-D, field, and bowhunting.

What If I Don't Classify But I Still Want To Shoot? What If I Need a Chair?
At most tournaments it won't be an issue, but you may want to call ahead and let the tournament director know. This way they may be able to make target assignments in such a way that you won't have to move on and off the line after every end. (This is a good idea for classified archers as well.) You will need to provide your own chair and it will need to fit into a regular shooting spot. If you need someone to pull your arrows, it is your responsibility to bring someone along to do that.

What If I Can't Pull My Own Arrows?
You can have someone else pull your arrows; that person is usually called an agent. Your agent can pull your arrows and can also represent you at the target. It's important to note though, that if you have an agent go to the target for you, you cannot go to the target. Sometimes the other archers on the target will pull your arrows for you, but when possible, it is a better idea to take your agent with you. Be aware though, that your agent will need a background check from USA Archery and they will need to take the SafeSport course. Information on both of these is on the USA Archery website.

Can I Shoot in a Para Category?
How Does Classification Work?
In order to shoot in a para category, you do need to be classified. Classification is usually offered once or twice a year, either at USA Archery tournaments or at events such as the Endeavor Games or Move United Nationals. Occasionally classifiers can meet you in their office or somewhere else and do the classification. For some athletes classification is pretty easy. For example, an amputation is pretty obvious and the classifier will not need to do other testing. However, for other archers it may be a longer (and occasionally painful) process. The classifiers may need to do muscle testing in order to decide how an archer should be classified.

Before the classification there will be medical forms (see *Resources*) and other forms that need to be completed and you will need to send a photo. In the USA, all of this is done through USA Archery. Once you are classified, be sure to always keep a copy of the classification form with your archery stuff - you will need it during equipment inspection. If's a good idea to keep a copy on your phone and a copy in a safe place.

Are There Rules Or Restrictions On Adaptive Equipment?

Yes there are, but you don't need to worry about them until you start competing. Your coach should be able to help you out. An important rule when you start competing is to make sure you and your equipment (including chairs and wheelchairs) will fit in the allotted space. When you are ready to be classified and ready to shoot in national tournaments, you will need to be aware of the rules. You can find the rules on the World Archery website. A link is included in the resource section.

Where Can I Get Adaptive Equipment?

Most equipment is standard archery equipment. It is usually not the archery equipment that is adapted, it has more to do with the way the bow is held or the arrow is released. A lot of it is custom made or made with the help of occupational therapists and prosthetists. You could check out the World Archery and USA Archery pages on YouTube. Look at the videos from the World Archery Para Championships and get some ideas, or check out USA Archery's Adaptive Archery series. You can also check out the articles in *Archery Focus* magazine. Other archers are usually happy to share their resources as well.

What About Anti-Doping Or The Medications I Take?

This is something to be aware of, but won't make a big difference until you start shooting national tournaments. Basically, there are some medicines and supplements that are not allowed during archery competitions because they can affect your performance. If you need to take one of the medications that is on the not-allowed list, there is a process you can go through to get a Therapeutic Use Exemption (TUE). Getting a TUE can take a while, so be sure to plan ahead. You can get more information at usantidoping.org

Do Kids Do Para-Archery? Do They Have Different Rules?

Most kids will do adaptive archery (see above) because they aren't classified. The rules are usually the same as they are for other kids. There are some clubs that run programs specifically for kids with disabilities, but most clubs in the USA will welcome kids with and without disabilities. This is the same for competitions. Some events, such as Move United's Junior Nationals are multi-sport events for young athletes with physical disabilities. The rules followed are very close to USA Archery's Junior Olympic (JOAD) rules, with a couple of minor variations.

Currently, USA Archery's JOAD program encourages kids with disabilities to shoot with the non-disabled kids in the appropriate age and equipment category. Recently, they have started including para categories at tournaments for youth, but the youths in the para categories must be classified.

If I Started Today Could I Make The 2024 Or 2028 Paralympic Games?

A lot of that depends on you and how hard you want to work! There is a common misconception that it's easy to make the Paralympic Archery team, you just need to have a disability and shoot a bow. If you've read the article to this point, you'll know that's not correct. Here's what I would suggest:

1. Find a coach and get started with regular lessons. Let the coach know your goal is the Paralympics so they steer you in the right direction as far as equipment and competitions.
2. Shoot local competitions and leagues if they are available. Come up with a regular practice schedule.
3. Learn about your equipment - and keep learning. Don't be afraid to tinker, but keep notes so you know what works and what doesn't. There's a lot of information on the internet, but you can probably learn more from your local archery pro-shop mechanics and from other archers. Be careful with internet information, not all of it is accurate.
4. Shoot more competitions and leagues and keep practicing. Make your practice deliberate, work on specific things and know what you are working on. A few good arrows shot is a lot better than many "flung" arrows. Practice up close so you can work on form. Remember good process will lead to better scores.
5. Get in touch with USA Archery and/or the National Coach and find out if there are any training camps you can attend. Find the USA Para Archery Facebook page and follow it so you know what's going on. Join USA Archery and get on their mailing list. The National Field Archery Association (NFAA) also does target tournaments, check them out too.
6. Start attending National tournaments. Find out when USA Archery will be offering classification and get it done as soon as you can. If you have it done at one of USA Archery's events, it will most likely be considered a "National" classification. That will be fine for USA events, but you will need to get an "International" classification. This has to be done at an international event. A National classifi-

cation will allow you to shoot in the para categories at USA Archery events.

7. Once you are classified and attending national tournaments, you can start being nationally ranked. This may change, but currently, if you are ranked in the top eight in your category and you have shot the Minimum Qualifying Score (MQS), and attended the necessary tournaments, you will be named to the National team. Benefits of being on the National team can include help with funding to some events and with some equipment.
8. There will be World Championships in 2025 and in 2027. There will also be other international events. Pay attention to your calendars and emails so you know the processes to shoot in the trials and make those teams. Some international events allow a limited amount of competitors and you have to earn a place at the trials; others have no limits and you can fund yourself if you don't make the team. Trials events are good practice, even it you don't make the team. If you haven't been internationally classified, the competitions with no limits on the numbers of athletes can be good opportunities to get classified, even if you have to self fund.
9. Shoot in the Paralympic trials, you'll either make the team or you won't. If you do, congratulations! If not, start over again and get ready for 2028, in the USA!

About the Author

Coach Randi Smith has worked as a Recreational Therapist, Adapted PE Teacher, and Family Crisis Therapist. These all seemed to be perfect preparation for becoming the Head Coach of the USA Paralympic Archery Team, which she took over in 2005.

Before taking the position as U.S. Para Archery Head Coach, she and her husband, Larry, also ran a very successful JOAD club, the Utah Hot Shots, as well as a full service archery shop. She and Larry taught thousands of beginners archery (over 35 years, 3-5 nights a week, 10 kids per class!), and many of them went on to become competitive archers. Together they certified more than 250 archery instructors. They also ran several national and regional tournaments.

She and Larry traveled all over the USA with their JOAD team. Randi traveled with Junior World Teams and with a college team. Randi was awarded the USA Archery Developmental Coach of the Year, the USA Paralympic Coach of the Year, and the Invictus Award three times.

During her time as the Para Archery Head Coach Randi's archers took at least 73 World, Pan American, and Paralympic medals, including 21 Gold Medals. She was named by her winning athletes to capture the Order of Ikkos Award, the highest honor for a coach, three separate times.

Randi Smith

A Short History of the Paralympics

The first organized athletic event for disabled athletes that coincided with the Olympic Games took place on the day of the opening of the 1948 Summer Olympics in London. Neurologist Sir Ludwig Guttmann of Stoke Mandeville Hospital, who had fled Nazi Germany with the help of the Council for Assisting Refugee Academics in 1939, hosted a sports competition for British World War 2 veteran patients with spinal cord injuries. The first games were called the 1948 International Wheelchair Games, and the Stoke Mandeville Games (amongst others) and were intended to coincide with the 1948 Olympics. Sixteen archers (both men and women) took part in the first competition Guttmann's aim was to create an elite sports competition for people with disabilities that would be equivalent to the Olympic Games. The games were held at the same location each year, and in 1952 Dutch and Israeli veterans took part alongside the British, making the Stoke Mandeville Games the first international competition of its own kind.

In 1960, the 9th annual games took place outside of the UK for the first time in Rome, to coincide with the 1960 Summer Olympics which were also being held in Rome. These were to be later designated the 1st Paralympic Games. These early competitions have been described as the precursors of the Paralympic Games, and Stoke Mandeville holds a similar place in the lore of the Paralympic movement as Greece holds in the Olympic movement.

The 1960 Games in Rome drew 400 athletes with disabilities from 23 countries, as proposed by doctor Antonio Maglio. As of the early 21st century, it is one of the largest international sporting events, with 4,520 athletes from 163 National Paralympic Committees at the 2020 Summer Paralympics. Since the 1988 Summer Olympics in Seoul, South Korea, all Paralympic Games are held almost immediately following the respective Olympic Games. All Paralympic Games are governed by the International Paralympic Committee (IPC).

The International Sport Organization for the Disabled (ISOD) was founded in 1964 and offered competition opportunities for disabled athletes who could not participate in the International Stoke Mandeville Games (ISMG). They included amputees, athletes with cerebral palsy, and paraplegics. The 1976 Games are the first to be fully recognized as Paralympic Games and not counted as International Stoke Mandeville Games.

In 1988 at the FITA World Championships, the sport specific classification system was introduced. It is still used (with many changes) today. The 1992 Paralympics in Barcelona were the first to include athletes with disabilities other than spinal cord injuries in the archery competition (https://www.paralympic.org/news/sport-week-history-para-archery).

In 1997, the International Stoke Mandeville Games became the World Wheelchair Games. In 2005 they were renamed the World Wheelchair and Amputee Games and in 2009 they became the International Wheelchair and Amputee Sports (IWAS) World Games. IWAS then merged with the Cerebral Palsy International Sports and Recreation Association (CPISRA) and is now World Abilitysport. The Worldability Sport Games offer both a developmental opportunity for new athletes and a chance for those with more experience to compete as they get ready for World Championships and Paralympics. The World Games and Youth Games are held in alternate years. They offer sports that are on the Paralympic Games program. They have Under 23, Open, and Masters (over 40years old) categories. They are recognized by IPC and continue to make a valuable contribution to Para sport.

The International Paralympic Committee (IPC) was founded in 1989 in Dusseldorf, Germany to act as the governing body of the Paralympic movement. The word "Paralympic" is from the Greek word "para" (alongside) and the word "Olympic." The Paralympics are parallel Games to the Olympics.

IPC was the governing body of para-archery until January 1, 2009 when it started the move to FITA (now World Archery). The move was completed later that year at the FITA Congress. Most international archery events (other than the Paralympic Games) are now governed by World Archery. In some countries (USA for example), para-archery is governed by the National Archery Governing Body; in other countries it is governed by their Paralympic Governing Body.

Archery has been and continues to be a part of all these organizations.

References

https://worldabilitysport.org/world-abilitysport-games/overview/
https://www.paralympic.org/news/sport-week-history-para-archery
https://en.wikipedia.org/wiki/IWAS_World_Games
https://www.paralympic.org/ipc/history

Resources

Adaptive Aids

- ***Active Hands*** activehands.com Gripping aids that hold the hands in a gripping shape. They also have many other adaptive aids.
- ***Fabtech Systems*** fabtechsystems.com Prosthetic components; have helped with shoulder releases
- ***GX4 Adaptive Archery*** https://gx4adaptivearchery.com
- ***Archery Shooter Systems*** www.bowhanger.com Maker of many kinds of bow stands, look under "NASP Approved" or "Indoor Hangers" for Archer Assist Stand.

Websites

(Note—Some of these websites are hard to navigate, so I included addresses to specific pages. *Randi*)

- ***Antidoping*** https://www.usada.org/
- ***Adaptive Sports Manual*** https://www.disabledsportsusa.org/sport/archery/
- ***Paralympics*** https://www.paralympic.org/
- ***Paralympics – Paris 2024*** https://www.paralympic.org/paris-2024
- ***Paralympic Qualifications*** https://www.paralympic.org/sites/default/files/2023-05/2023_0512 Paris QR_v1.5.5.pdf
- ***World Archery*** https://www.worldarchery.sport/
- ***World Archery Para Archery*** https://www.worldarchery.sport/sport/disciplines/para-archery
- ***World Archery Para Archery Classification*** https://www.worldarchery.sport/sport/disciplines/para-archery/classification
- ***World Archery Para Archery Rules*** https://www.worldarchery.sport/rulebook/article/82
- ***World Archery Adaptive Equipment Resource Guide*** https://extranet.worldarchery.sport/documents/index.php/?doc=5897
- ***USA Archery*** https://www.usarchery.org/
- ***USA Archery Adaptive Archery*** https://www.usarchery.org/par-

ticipate/adaptive-archery

- ***USA Archery Classification*** https://www.usarchery.org/participate/adaptive-archery/para-archery-classification
- ***"Making the U.S. Paralympic Archery Team"*** https://www.usarchery.org/high-performance/making-the-us-paralympic-archery-team
- ***USA Archery International Team Selection Procedures*** https://www.usarchery.org/resource-center/high-performance/athlete-internationa-team-selection-procedures
- ***Move United*** https://moveunitedsport.org/
- ***Move United Sport Locator*** https://moveunitedsport.org/locations/
- ***Move United Events*** https://moveunitedsport.org/events/
- ***The Move United Junior Nationals*** (www.moveunited.com)
- ***The Endeavor Games*** (www.moveunited.com)
- ***The National Veterans' Wheelchair Games*** (https://wheelchairgames.org/)
- ***The Warrior Games*** (https://dodwarriorgames.com)
- ***The Invictus Games*** (https://invictusgamesfoundation.org)
- ***Headstrong Consulting*** (headstrongconsulting.com) They also have a podcast called "Becoming Headstrong"
- ***USOPC Coaching Education*** https://www.teamusa.org/ About-the-USOPC/Coaching-Education
- ***Visually Impaired Archery*** www.seenolimits.org
- ***British Blind Sport-Archery*** https://britishblindsport.org.uk/membership/bbs-sports/archery/

Videos

- ***Adaptive Archery Video Series*** https://www.youtube.com/playlist?list=PLK7QwuzL25xm8yOglKjbFlc2Rt0whPpSw
- ***Positive Coaching Alliance*** https://positivecoach.org/
- ***YouTube*** (There are lots and lots and lots of how to archery videos on YouTube. These are my favorites and have good information. *Randi*)

  Online Archery Academy
  Korea Archery Academy
  How to Coach Archery: Archery GB
  USA Archery Adapted Archery Series

Books

General Books I'd Recommend to Start

- ***Mindset: The New Psychology of Success*** by Carol Dweck Ph,D.
- ***The Motivation Myth*** by Jeff Haden
- ***The Culture Code*** by Daniel Coyle
- ***The Little Book of Talent*** by Daniel Coyle
- ***Unconventional Coaching: A Research Based Approach to Coaching*** by John Leonzo

Archery Specific Books

(Note—These are archery specific books. One thing you'll notice (if you haven't already) is that there are lots of ways to shoot archery! There are definitely some basic concepts - but there is definitely not one right way. Find what works and aim for consistency and repeatability. Doing it the same every time is what you need to learn to teach and to do. *Randi*)

Favorites

- ***Coaching Archery for Beginning to Intermediate Coaches*** by Steve Ruis
- ***The Simple Art of Winning: How to Shoot Your Best*** by Rick McKinney
- ***Archery Fundamentals: All You Need to Know to Aim, Shoot, and Score*** by Teresa Johnson
- ***Choose to Be a Winner*** by Jens Fudge
- ***Planning to Peak in Archery*** by Larry Wise
- ***The Archery Drill Book*** by Steve Ruis and Mike Gerard
- ***Don't Leave the Mind Behind*** by Keith Henschen and Nicole Detling

Other Archery Books

(Note—All of these books contain good information. Some are more detailed, some are more philosophical, and some are more advanced. Randi)

- ***Archery for Beginners*** by John C. Williams
- ***Total Archery: Inside the Archer*** by Kisik Lee and Tyler Benner
- ***Archery*** by Coach Kim Hyung Tak
- ***The Competitive Archer*** by Simon Needham
- ***The Heretic Archer*** by Vittorio & Michele Frangilli
- ***Archery Anatomy*** by Ray Axford

- ***Core Archery: Shooting with Proper Back Tension*** by Larry Wise
- ***Advanced Archer: How to Stay Calm at the Center*** by Thomas Whitney & Vishnu Karmakar
- ***One Arrow, One Life: Zen, Archery, and Daily Life*** by Kenneth Kushner
- ***Sports Medicine and Science in Archery*** Edited by Emin Ergen & Karol Hibner
- ***Denise Parker: A Teenage Archer's Quest for Olympic Glory*** by Denise Parker
- ***A Sport for Everyone: Archery*** by The Athletic Institute
- ***Zen in the Art of Archery*** by Eugen Herrigel
- ***Archery Fundamentals: A Better Way to Learn the Basics*** by Douglas Engh
- ***Archery*** by Wayne C. McKinney
- ***Peak Performance Archery*** by Al Henderson
- ***Training for Archery*** by Jake Kaminski
- ***Archery: The Ultimate Resource for Recurve and Compound Archers*** by USA Archery
- ***Modern Recurve Tuning: Start to Finish*** by Richard A. Cockrell
- ***The Witchery of Archery*** by Maurice Thompson

For Even More Information

(Note—These books are more general coaching information. I've found all of them to be valuable. *Randi*)

- ***Positive Coaching*** by Jim Thompson
- ***In Pursuit of Excellence*** by Terry Orlick
- ***The Talent Code*** by Daniel Coyle
- ***The Chimp Paradox*** by Steve Peters
- ***Practice Perfect*** by Doug Lemov, Erica Woolway, Katie Yezzi
- ***Golf is Not a Game of Perfect*** by Bob Rotella
- ***Inside Out Coaching*** by Joe Ehrmann
- ***The Power Of Moments*** by Chip Heath and Dan Heath
- ***Coaching Better Every Season*** by Wade Gilbert
- ***Every Moment Matters*** by John O'Sullivan
- ***Chatter*** by Ethan Kross
- ***Talent is Overrated*** by Geoff Calvin
- ***What Did You Say? The Art of Giving and Receiving Feedback*** by Charles Seashore, Gerald M. Weinberg, Edith W. Seashore
- ***The Practicing Mind*** by Thomas M. Sterner
- ***Thanks for the Feedback*** by Douglas Stone, Sheila Teen

- ***The Essential Wooden*** by John Wooden, Steve Jamison
- ***Raise Your Game*** by Alan Stein Jr., Jon Sternfeld
- ***Coaching Excellence*** by Frank Pyke
- ***Grit*** by Angela Duckworth
- ***The Sports Gene*** by David Epstein
- ***You Haven't Taught Until They've Learned***: John Wooden's Teaching Principles and Practice by Sven Nater
- ***Range: Why Generalists Triumph in a Specialized World*** by David Epstein
- ***Drive: The Surprising Truth about What Motivates Us*** by Daniel Pink
- ***Atomic Habits: An Easy & Proven Way to Build Good Habits & Break Bad Ones*** by James Clear
- ***35 Secrets of Brilliant Coaches*** (article) https://annejosephson.wordpress.com/2014/07/14/30-secrets-of-brilliant-coaches/

Lists

Reference Medical Form

https://americandisabledarchers.com/page-17/ or
RandisRecreation.com

Here is some assistance in filling out the medical forms in the classification process.

Tournament Accessibility Checklist
(con't)

Tournament Accessibility Checklist

Yes	With help	No		Notes - We'd hope that National tournaments would be totally accessible and be able to check "yes" on everything below. For smaller, local tournaments, working towards a "yes" on everything could be a reasonable goal.
			Field Access	
				Is there enough designated accessible parking?
				Does the designated parking allow space and level ground for vans with lifts?
				Can athletes get to the field from the parking area?
				Is the distance from the parking area to the field reasonable?
				Can athletes get their equipment to the field (or is there help)?
				Can athletes get to the area where they turn in scorecards?
				If there is an emergency, can athletes get off the field quickly?
				Is there access for emergency vehicles and services?
			On the Field	
				Can athletes get everywhere they might need to get?
				Registration and equipment check in areas?
				Their shooting spot?
				Water stations and get water?
				Restrooms?
				Concession and vending areas?
				Out of the weather if necessary?
				Have target assignments been made so that athletes with wheelchairs or stools can stay on the line?
			Awards	
				Can athletes get to the awards area?
				Is the award stand accessible to archers in wheelchairs or with mobility issues?
				If not, can you come up with something else or fix it?
			Restroom s	
				Are there enough accessible restrooms?
				Can athletes get to the restrooms and back in a reasonable time?
				Can athletes get the restroom doors open so they can get in and out?
			Concessi ons	
				If seating is provided, are there spots for people using wheelchairs?
			Banquets or Social Events	
				Is the speakers' stand accessible to all speakers and archers?

Athlete and Coach Travel Packing Lists

These packing lists are the lists I provided to coaches and athletes before we left on a trip.

Some items were required, others suggested. There were some that needed to go in a carry on, including everything they'd need for 24-48 hours in case their luggage were delayed. (I'd now recommend they get trackers and put them in their luggage so it can be traced if necessary.)

I had every athlete bring a roll of duct tape, and we used some on every trip.

Being prepared for issues with portable toilets was important. We had events where the portable toilets ran out of toilet paper and sometimes they weren't really clean. Disinfecting wipers were handy for cleaning; body wipes were nice when we ran out of toilet paper. I also recommended they keep a roll of toilet paper in their bow case. Hand sanitizer comes in handy after portable toilet uses, too.

Many international tournaments how provide all information electronically, so its important that your device not run out of power. Portable power banks can keep you supplied with power.

Ziploc bags in all sizes were used, also. The "sandwich" size could be used to pack a snack from breakfast. Larger ones could be used for ice or to keep things dry in our cooler (if we had one). I did occasionally use a cooler as one of my luggage "bags." It worked well and then we did have a cooler on the field, although finding ice was sometimes a challenge.

(con't)

Athlete Checklist

Key Req. Int. = Required International; Sug. Int. = Suggested International; Nat. = National

Req Int.	Sug. Int.	Nat.	Packed	Item	Notes
☑	☐	☐	☐	Passport (leave copy at home)	
	☑	☐	☐	Credit card (leave copy at home)	recommended
☑	☐	☑	☐	Classification card (or paper)	have copy on phone as well
☐	☐	☑	☑	USA Archery Membership card	
☑	☐	☑	☐	Team uniform	one in carry on
☑	☐	☑	☐	Layering under clothes	
☑	☐	☐	☐	Track jacket and pants	part of uniform
☑	☐	☐	☐	Rain jacket and pants	no specific gear
☑	☐	☐	☐	Shooting shoes	
☑	☐	☐	☐	Extra pair of shoes	in your carryon
☑	☐	☐	☐	Umbrella	for rain and sun
☑	☐	☐	☐	Personal medications	
☐	☑	☐	☐	Outfit for Final Party	casual barbecue attire
☐	☑	☐	☐	Clothes for relaxing/touristing	no USA markings
☐	☑	☐	☐	Pajamas, socks, and underwear	
☐	☑	☐	☐	Swimsuit	if the hotel has a pool
☐	☑	☐	☐	Soap, shampoo, toothpaste/brush, etc.	
☐	☑	☐	☐	Toilet paper and/or wipes	sometimes int. sites are lacking
☐	☑	☐	☐	Your own towel and/or pillowcase	unique so they don't match hotel's
☐	☑	☐	☐	Gloves	
☐	☑	☐	☐	Hand warmers	
☐	☑	☐	☐	Earplugs	highly recommended
☐	☑	☐	☐	Regular glasses	
☐	☑	☐	☐	Sunglasses	
☐	☑	☐	☐	Windup or battery aleam clock	
☐	☑	☐	☐	Hand sanitizer & disinfecting wipes	in your bow case
☑	☐	☐	☐	Sharpie or permanent marker	
☑	☐	☐	☐	Lock for bowcase	
☑	☐	☐	☐	Duct tape	everyone bring a roll
☑	☐	☐	☐	Extra nocks, fletches, glue, etc.	
☑	☐	☐	☐	Arrow puller and lube	
☑	☐	☐	☐	Other repair and back-up parts	
☑	☐	☐	☐	Any needed bathroom supplies	
☑	☐	☐	☐	Footrests	for those who need them
☑	☐	☐	☐	Wheelchair repair parts	for those who might need them
☐	☐	☐	☐	Microfiber/absorbant towels	nice if it rains
☐	☐	☐	☐	Power converters and adapters	
☐	☐	☐	☐	Chargers for things that need them	
☐	☐	☐	☐	Snacks, energy bars, water flavorings	
☐	☐	☐	☐	Entertainments (books, music, etc.)	for non-shooting times
☐	☐	☐	☐	Trading items	

Carry On Stuff

ð	|	|	|	Passport, printed copy of itinerary	
ð	|	|	|	Medications	in prescription bottles
ð	|	|	|	48 hours worth of clothes, pers. hygiene stuff	
ð	|	|	|	One complete shooting uniform	shirt and shorts
ð	|	|	|	USA track jacket	
|	|	|	|	Entertainments (books, music, etc.)	
|	|	|	|	Snacks, refillable water bottle	

Coaches Checklist

Key Req. Int. = Required International; Sug. Int. = Suggested International; Nat. = National

Req Int.	Sug. Int.	Nat.	Packed	Item	Notes
☑	☐	☑	☐	Clothes for layering	in case of bad weather
☑	☐	☑	☐	Uniform	
☑	☐	☑	☐	Competition shoes	
☑	☐	☐	☐	Extra pair of shoes	
☑	☐	☐	☐	Nice outfit for banquet	
☑	☐	☐	☐	Outfit for touristing	no USA markings
☑	☐	☐	☐	Passport (bring a copy, leave one at home)	
☑	☐	☐	☐	Refillable water bottle	
☑	☐	☐	☐	Extra socks and underwear	
☑	☐	☐	☐	USAA rain jacket and pants	
☑	☐	☐	☐	USAA track jacket and pants	
☑	☐	☐	☐	24 hours of neccesities (toothbrush, etc.)	in carry on bag
☑	☐	☐	☐	Medications (in original containers)	
☑	☐	☐	☐	One uniform set	in carry on bag
☐	☑	☐	☐	Appeal form	
☐	☑	☐	☐	Arrow pullers and lube	for you and the coaches
☐	☑	☐	☐	Battery alarm clock	in case power goes out
☐	☑	☐	☐	Bungie cords	
☐	☑	☑	☐	Copies of classification forms	(electronic in USA)
☐	☑	☐	☐	Door stop	so I could keep my door open
☐	☑	☐	☐	Duct tape	
☐	☑	☐	☐	Extra batteries	
☐	☑	☑	☐	Chargeable portable power blocks	
☐	☑	☐	☐	FITA rules	can be electronic
☐	☑	☐	☐	Flashlight	in case power goes out
☐	☑	☐	☐	Gifts for tournament people	small gifts to say thank you
☐	☑	☐	☐	Golf tees	as toe markers, target pins, etc.
☐	☑	☐	☐	Large garbage bags	to cover things if it rains
☐	☑	☐	☐	Letter of invitation to event	printed and in your carry on bag
☐	☑	☑	☐	Microfiber towels	for drying equipment
☐	☑	☐	☐	USA flag	
☐	☑	☐	☐	Blank targets for signing	
☐	☑	☐	☐	Backpack (in suitcase)	eases carrying stuff to field
☐	☑	☑	☐	Alligator clips	keeps clothes out of the way
☐	☑	☐	☐	Zip ties	

☐ ☑ ☐ ☐ Office supplies — in a small box for order

Personal Stuff

☐ ☐ ☐ ☐ MP3 player, books, etc.
☐ ☐ ☐ ☐ Personal business cards
☐ ☐ ☐ ☐ Personal items — shampoo, toothpaste, etc.
☐ ☐ ☐ ☐ Hats (for sun and cold)
☐ ☐ ☐ ☐ Power converters/adapters/charging cables, etc.
☐ ☐ ☐ ☐ Schedule
☐ ☐ ☐ ☐ Ear plugs
☐ ☐ ☐ ☐ Silver pens (Sharpies)
☐ ☐ ☐ ☐ Snacks
☐ ☐ ☐ ☐ Sunglasses
☐ ☐ ☐ ☐ Umbrella
☐ ☐ ☐ ☐ Hand sanitizer/wipes

These lists worked well for me. Obviously there will be some changes to fit your situation. If we were going to an event where we knew things we forgot could be easily obtained, there wasn't as much pressure than in the opposite case. Some things, like duct tape and garbage bags, I learned about from experience!

Made in United States
Troutdale, OR
08/20/2023

12227648R00117